Owl Sight

Evidence-Based Discernment and the Promise of Organizational Intelligence for Ministry

J. Russell Crabtree

Magi Press

Endorsements

Owl Sight brings great clarity to the topic of evidence-based discernment which is a distinguishing feature of Crabtree's work. Leaders in churches, regional associations, and church-related colleges and schools will find *Owl Sight* to be a powerful tool for helping them understand how people in their organi-zations actually think and feel. As a former college dean responsible for assessing organizational vitality and improvement, I wish I had had Russ Crabtree as my consultant. As a current church consultant, I am able to lead my clients to significant self-understanding because I use his assessment tools. For those of us who care about the future of faith-based organizations, *Owl Sight* is a lamp unto our feet.

James L. Pence, Ph.D.

"This superb book by J. Russell Crabtree invites readers to a new way of thinking about the promise for organizational intelligence through the use of proven scientific tools of research made easy to use. This book is alive with information and insights with the kind of resourceful approach to understanding congregations and how to develop their renewal and vitality. Russ Crabtree teaches and demonstrates that congregations can and will benefit from regular and ongoing survey of their landscape.

This is arguably the most influential work on congregational organizational intelligence that is available today. Russ Crabtree is one of the most perceptive writers of congregational development and vitality. This is important reading for any pastor, lay leader or denominational leader interested in understanding how congregation members are experiencing their faith communities. Without this kind of data, congregations are simply doing strategic planning in the dark."

Susan T. Czolgosz

"Russ Crabtree's new book *Owl Sight* not only gives voice to a new and dependable approach to growing leaders and congregations, it offers a vision of real change that happens from the inside out. Evidence-based discernment and "organizational intelligence" is about meeting us where we are, but not leaving us there and an unwavering understanding that every voice is a God given gift and guide."

Keith Magnuson, Principal Owner, Kairos and Associates, Inc.

"*Owl Sight* enables congregational leadership to leverage information for the greatest Kingdom impact. This work clearly demonstrates how the anecdotally based decisions that most congregations use result in haphazard mission and derail a congregation's desire to become more healthy and vital. This book is good news for all churches that have tried and failed to transform. It both illustrates why so many plans fail and provides a clear path that will leverage a congregation's gifts. *Owl Sight* successfully merges the insights of organizational theory, foundational theological principles, and accessibility for its readers. I highly recommend this book to anyone seeking to navigate the challenge of being Church in the 21st century."

Dr. Tom Evans, Presbytery executive, Presbytery of Greater Atlanta

OWL SIGHT
Evidence-Based Discernment and the Promise
of Organizational Intelligence for Ministry

Holy Cow! Consulting
PO Box 8422
Columbus, Ohio 43201

Publishing consultant: Huff Publishing Associates, LLC

ISBN 978-0-615-64596-4

Cover images: Dreamstime.com
Cover and interior design: Marti Naughton

To Shawn K. Kelly,
wife and Galway girl

Contents

Acknowledgments

In the acknowledgments for my book *Fly in the Ointment,* I indicated that the book had roughly fifty thousand contributors. For this book, that number is now seventy thousand. As was the case then, the vast majority of these must remain unnamed because the contribution was an anonymous though very personal sharing of their thoughts through a series of questions they chose to answer. This makes it difficult to speak in any possessive way about the discoveries in this book. It is not so much what I have discovered but what we have discovered together.

However, in the midst of a multitude too great to number, a few names are important to mention. I want to thank Bill Huff, owner of Huff Publishing Associates for ably shepherding this book to completion, Andrea Lee for her thorough and extremely helpful editing of the material, and Marti Naughton for the terrific cover design.

It is always important to have the support of critical thinkers who will read early versions of a manuscript, make invaluable suggestions, and then take their place squarely in your corner. These precious folks include James Pence, Rev. Rebecca McClain, Susan Czolgosz, and Tom Evans. I am especially grateful for Keith Magnuson and Jeff Kjellberg for carrying the work of organizational intelligence into the fields of financial campaigns and church camps.

A special thanks goes to Robyn Strain, who managed many of the details and source discovery for this book at a time when my ability to do so was totally depleted.

My wife, Shawn, inspires me as a skilled manager in health care where she uses evidence-based approaches to make the treatment of children as effective and painless as possible. Somehow, she continues to read what I write and offer tireless support. Though they are now some distance from us, leaders in our spiritual communities continue to be important in our thinking, especially Rev. George Glazier of St. Stephen's Episcopal Church and Father Vinny McKiernan of the Newman Center in Columbus, Ohio.

When I think that all these gifts are expressions of the pure grace of God, I run out of words.

Introduction

They came to Bethsaida, and some people brought a blind man and begged Jesus to touch him. He took the blind man by the hand and led him outside the village. When he had spit on the man's eyes and put his hands on him, Jesus asked, "Do you see anything?" He looked up and said, "I see people; they look like trees walking around."

—Mark 8:22–24

In contrast to other successful organizations today, as a whole, the leadership team of a typical congregation is generally clueless regarding how the members they lead are experiencing the church. This is not a criticism. The world has changed and church leaders have not yet realized the possibilities now available to them. Nonetheless, this level of confusion is having a subtle yet devastating impact upon nearly every significant decision leaders make. In addition, church members are baffled by what is happening to their churches as they watch an inexorable cycle of debilitating episodes play out in their congregations over and over again, not realizing the factors that are driving those patterns can be clearly identified and remedied. I believe that evidence-based discernment processes hold real promise for the leaders and members of faith communities. In this book I examine these current realities for churches and propose ways in which evidence-based discernment can help them move to healthier and more effective ways of being the church today.

What Leaders in Hospitals, Libraries, and Coffee Shops Know

Three years ago I worked as a consultant to a hospital where my wife served as the director of one of the busiest pediatric emergency departments in the United States. Each year, the department treats about eighty thousand children with problems ranging from the common cold to the trauma of a

1

horrific car crash. On average, the parents wait with their children about an hour before the child is seen by a physician, longer in some cases, less in true emergencies. By the time they are treated and ready to walk out the door (if they are not admitted), they have spent about three hours of their day in the emergency department.

The department is staffed by about two hundred people who are managed by a twelve-member clinical leader team. It is organizationally complex. I asked my wife this question: "If you were to sit down with your clinical leader team and ask the twelve of them to estimate the percentage of parents walking out the door who are clearly satisfied with their experience of the emergency department, what would be the *range* of their estimates?"

In spite of the variables and complexity of the work dealing with thousands of children and hundreds of workers, her answer was clear: 75 to 85 percent. (See figure I-1.)

Figure I-1. Range of Estimates of Patient Satisfaction
by a Twelve-Member Clinical Team (Percent)

I have also worked as a consultant to a large number of public libraries in my career. I know from my experience that if I asked the leadership team of a public library to estimate the percentage of patrons in their community who are clearly satisfied with their experience of the library, their *range* of estimates would be 85 to 95 percent. (See figure I-2.) In fact, one librarian said, "We don't do surveys anymore. Everybody loves us!"

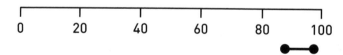

Figure I-2. Range of Estimates of Patron Satisfaction
by a Library Team (Percent)

My third example of what other organizations know comes from my son-in-law, who is the president of a coffee company that has about a dozen coffee shops in Columbus, Ohio. Each shop has a store manager, and he meets with all his store managers as a team every week. By now, you know the question I asked him. "If you were to sit down with your store managers and ask them to estimate the percentage of customers walking out the door who are clearly satisfied with their experience of one of your coffee shops, what would be the *range* of their estimates?"

Since he is in the food-service business, his rating system is a little different. They use stars, as in a "five-star restaurant."

He said, "Four and a half to five stars."

What Church Leaders Usually Know

When I ask the leaders of a typical church, board members and staff, to estimate what percentage of members are clearly satisfied with what is happening in their church, the range of the estimates given by a typical leadership team is generally from 40 to 90 percent. (See figure I-3.)

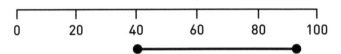

Figure I-3. Range of Estimates of Member Satisfaction
by a Church Leadership Team (Percent)

When I ask these leaders to estimate what percentage of members would say that the church has a sense of energy and excitement as opposed to people simply going through the motions, the range of estimates is from 20 to 100 percent. (See figure I-4.)

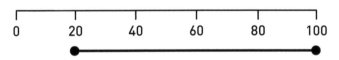

Figure I-4. Range of Estimates of Energy
by a Church Leadership Team (Percent)

I repeat: this is a typical church. I see the same results from the leaders of churches across the country. In conducting this research, I get frustrated responses from some leaders and messages like, "I have no idea how members would respond to such questions. How am I supposed to know that?" It is not immediately apparent to them why it is significant that the owner of their local coffee shop knows more about the experiences of their members than they do. And he or she is just selling coffee.

There is no reason to believe that any group of a dozen members would do any better than their leaders at estimating the quality of experience that their fellow members as a whole are having in the church. It is the classic tale of the elephant and the blind men, except members are guessing about the church not through what they are touching but by the various groups they happen to be part of. Since members have no clear picture of the church as a whole, they also have no idea which approaches are likely to bear fruit and which are likely dead ends. They also have no insight into the overall patterns of behavior that are repeatedly sabotaging their best efforts. Their only option is to *react* to the leadership (rather than *follow* the leadership) based on their vague perception of where the church is. I am convinced that part of the reason we have churches with reactive members is this lack of clarity. Following a leader when neither you nor the leader knows where the trail begins is difficult.

It feels "normal" to most church leaders not to have a clear understanding of member perspectives, experiences, and aspirations. I will leave it to you to reflect on why it is that congregational leaders have normalized a kind of organizational agnosticism or information vacuum at a time when other successful organizations are investing a significant amount of energy and resources to measure their impact upon those they serve. Whether we like it or not, we live in an age of Wikileak transparency and customized coupon clarity.

In a prophetic 2012 article regarding organizational intelligence, *New York Times* writer Steve Lohr puts it this way:

> The story is similar in fields as varied as science and sports, advertising and public health—a drift toward data-driven discovery and decision-making. "It's a revolution," says Gary King, director of Harvard's Institute for Quantitative Social Science. "We're really just getting under way. But the march of quantification, made possible by enormous new sources of data, will sweep through academia, business and government. There is no area that is going to be untouched."[1]

Unfortunately, when it comes to "organizational intelligence," that is, understanding the perspectives and relational patterns of the people they are called to lead and serve, most church leaders are seeing men and women as trees walking—like the blind man in the healing story from Mark 8—and this is making their work harder, less effective, and therefore less satisfying. More important, congregations are losing out to other organizations that spend far more time and energy understanding the people they want to influence, often in directions running perpendicular to the values of the kingdom of God.

In fact, investing in the tools needed to obtain clarity feels "abnormal" to leaders at first; most have not had the experience before. In nearly every church that undertakes a step into clarity, I hear leaders indicating a liberation that they did not think was possible. As one leader put it after getting his first glimpse of organizational intelligence from his church, "It feels like I've been taking a test for three years and I finally got a glimpse of the answer sheet!"

What Difference Does Confusion Make?

So what? What difference does confusion make? For those of us who are called to lead churches into health and vitality, lack of clarity makes a difference in every significant decision we make. Let's take a closer look at the information provided by the leaders of the church above, which we will refer to as St. Anywhere.

The leaders of St. Anywhere are seeing at least two very different churches. If the leaders who estimated that 90 percent of members are clearly satisfied and 100 percent of members are clearly energized are correct, *this is one of the most vibrant churches in the United States.*

- *Strategically,* this church needs to engage in efforts related to growth, expansion, replication, and external impact.
- *The pastor* needs to focus on ways to leverage the church's exceptional energy for the purposes of the kingdom, including activities such as strategizing, mentoring, teaching, and succession planning.
- *The people* need to be encouraged to move beyond core, internal ministries, take additional risks, and explore a variety of avenues for taking their faith into the world.

On the other hand, if the leaders who estimated that only 40 percent of members of St. Anywhwere are clearly satisfied and only 20 percent of members are clearly energized are correct, *this church is in trouble.*

- *Strategically,* this church needs to develop a vision that can lead to revitalization and renewal of its people and ministries.
- *The pastor* may need to evaluate whether this church is really a good fit for his or her gifts and discern whether the time has come to move on to another call.
- *The people* may need to turn their attention to the core curriculum of being a church and the basics of Christian worship, ministry, relationships, and spiritual practice.

Virtually none of the approaches to ministry that will work in the first view of St. Anywhere will work in the second view of St. Anywhere. Most important, if this latter set of leaders is correct, this church cannot grow. To grow a church where members, by their own admission, are generally unhappy and lack clear purpose is next to impossible. In fact, one could make the case that it is immoral to bring new people into a church with the predictable result that, after a short-lived burst of positive energy, they will become just as demoralized as everyone else. Jesus reserved his most stinging rebukes for evangelistic efforts that bring people into an experience that not only fails to liberate them but also burdens them further (Luke 11:46). If the more sober estimate of this latter group of leaders is correct, the church has no business trying to reach new members with the good news until they can demonstrate in their corporate life the truth they are proclaiming.

This murky understanding of where the church is and what it should do not only makes it difficult for leaders to lead; it also makes it almost impossible for members to know how to follow. Member perceptions of the church are largely shaped by a small group of relationships that may or may not reflect the larger body. The only time they do have an opportunity to get a sense of the body as a whole is at congregational meetings, where they generally hear one conflicting voice after another offering his or her rendering of the state of the church.

The issue here is not simply the egocentric question of who is right and who is wrong. The issue is "Which church is it?" Collectively, the leaders in the boardroom do not know. The answer does not exist around that table. If they do not know which church it is, they do not know what to do next, and members do not know whom to follow. We can see how debilitating this confusion can be to every part of the church and its mission.

In fact, no consultant, denominational representative, or other external resource that takes their cue from the leadership alone—or any small group of members—knows what to do next either. Their only option is to apply a one-size-fits-all approach that often leaves people more demoralized when it does not produce the expected results.

Which Church Is It?

Although a political decision can be forced in one direction or another using Robert's Rules of Order, no amount of debating and voting by leaders will answer the question "Which church is it?" No amount of political process will answer that question. I consider myself to be a fairly good facilitator, but no amount of facilitation, however skilled, will get to this answer. A leadership team cannot brainstorm its way to the answer. Interviews of staff and board members will not get to this answer. Storytelling will not get to this answer either.

Some might say, "But on average, leaders probably get it right." Actually, in critical areas they often do not. I have had situations where leaders, on average, think satisfaction and energy is twice as high as it actually is. As a result, they tend to make decisions in favor of the status quo when a deteriorating morale would argue for a more aggressive change strategy instead.

Even if leaders do get it right on average, it is a little bit like a man who has one foot in a pail of boiling water and the other foot in a pail of ice water. On average, he is comfortable! But is he? The problem with average as a statistical tool is that it obscures what is happening on the edges. A church where everyone agrees that the pastor is an adequate preacher is very different from one where half the people think the pastor is a great preacher and the other half think the pastor is a lousy preacher, even though the average is the same. The lack of clarity results in paralysis, conflict, strategic and tactical errors, poor pastoral fit, leader burnout, and threshold losses (losses that drop churches below a sustainable threshold, such as affording pastoral staff).

Putting it another way, when leaders wonder what the temperature is outside, they can take a vote on the temperature outside, brainstorm the temperature outside, interview one another about the temperature outside, or tell stories about a time when the temperature outside was really nice. Or they can carry a thermometer outside, take the temperature, and then spend their best energy planning how to make it a great day.

That's what this book is about: delivering leaders and members from the guesswork of deliberation so that they can pour more of their energy into the soul work of imagination and inspiration. Is that not our birthright? Is that not why we leaders jumped into this work in the first place? Is this not what we as members want from those who lead us?

Owl Sight: The Promise of Clarity

I have worked as a consultant for more than twenty years. I have listened to the perceptions, experiences, and aspirations of thousands of members and worked with hundreds of churches and scores of regional associations. I have also consulted with public libraries, hospitals, schools, and universities. What all these have in common with churches is that they are all organizations. Today, there are basically two kinds of organizations: (1) those with leaders who have clarity about who they are, what they are called to do, and how well they are doing it, and (2) those who do not. My experience is that most churches fall into the second category, not for want of good people but for lack of tools and information.

This book makes the argument that *how leaders choose to collect information will determine what is visible and invisible in their discernment processes, will fundamentally define their leadership experience and impact, and will be decisive in shaping the church that develops under their leadership.* I am calling this quality of leadership that has broken through to a greater level of clarity "owl sight." The name springs from my penchant for alliances with the natural world and the remarkable visual acuity of owls. They have enormous eyes for their body weight, a wide, binocular, 3D field of vision, a head that can rotate 270 degrees as well as turn itself nearly upside down, a densely packed retina anchored to the bones in the head and consisting mostly of rods feeding into an advanced neural pattern-recognition system. All of this enables the owl to see what is totally invisible to most other animals. I was also amused to discover in a word search of this text that *owl* is imbedded in the word *knowledge*.

While an owl gains the visual advantage through sight, organizational intelligence is developed through assessments. Throughout the book, I have generally sought to avoid the word *survey* and opt for *assessment* instead. In the politically charged atmosphere in which we live, *survey* carries the baggage of a referendum or approval rating. As we shall see, this one dimensional impression is as distant from organizational intelligence as an X-ray is from a coloring book. It is this misunderstanding that generates anxiety and resistance in leaders who usually experience a real assessment as liberating and confidence building.

Owl sight promises a different leadership experience for pastors and lay leaders that is based a deeper level of understanding. Owl sight encompasses not only collecting and seeing information but also using it to imagine what is possible for their organization. It can be of benefit to pastors, lay leaders, and members in the following ways.

For Pastors

- Developing more clarity about who they are, the kinds of churches that are a good fit for them, which churches are not, and which churches will run their self-confidence through a buzz saw.
- Providing them with the leverage to do what is best for the entire church when a narrowly focused minority besets them with complaints, inevitably ending with the coda "And we are not the only ones who feel this way."
- Lasering in on the training and professional development that will be most beneficial for them and their churches, thereby making their ministries more fruitful and fulfilling.
- Identifying the no-win catch-22s that are often part and parcel of church cultures *before* they snag the trip wire.
- Focusing on what needs to be done now and what can and should wait until the next phase . . . or never.
- Accurately gauging capacity in order to know when to push, when to give people a rest, and when to let a good thing go.

For Lay Leaders

- Developing a greater sense of unity in the leadership team, because long debates about where the church is and what members are actually thinking are eliminated.

- Having more productive discretionary time, because the focus is on the issues that are likely to have the biggest "pop for the clock."
- Opening up opportunities in other parts of the body of Christ for spiritual development, team building, training, creativity, and discovery of best practices.
- Avoiding failure paths, paved by cliché, that turn out to be fictions that have no support in reality and end up wasting time and energy. Great leaders love dead-end signs.
- Calling clergy that click with them, who not only have the *chemistry* but also the critical *ability* to lead in their particular context.
- Setting out a vision for the congregation that is appropriate and promising for reaching their community rather than a fantasy based upon an outdated, unrealistic, and sentimental wish for a once-upon-a-time church.

For Members

- Generating a higher level of confidence in the decisions that leaders make, because they understand that those decisions are being made with 20/20 clarity about the church as a whole.
- Having a clear rationale from congregational leaders when they recommend changes, which makes even difficult changes easier to accept.
- Being able to respond to disruptive and sometimes dysfunctional voices that are promulgating a view of the church that is neither accurate nor productive.

The Journey of Owl Sight

As with most books, this book will take you on a journey. As with any journey, you cannot skip the first step because all subsequent steps build on the first. Therefore, I encourage you to take the four parts in order.

Part 1 lays out the foundations for owl sight, beginning with the definitions of organizational intelligence and evidence-based discernment in chapter 1. Evidence-based discernment is presented as an alternative to what most leaders are experiencing today in their decision making, an approach that integrates information and kingdom values rather than treating them as opposites. As Jesus makes clear in his ministry, sight requires a willingness to see. Therefore, part 1 also addresses the preparation required for seeing: a willingness to trust our instruments, an openness to surprises, and a recognition of the inevitable temptations and spiritual obstacles that always line the path to greater self-awareness.

With those preparations made, part 2 launches into the structure of organizational intelligence, what it discloses and what it makes possible. Many leaders come to the subject of organizational intelligence expecting to see a two-dimensional political snapshot of what people are for and against. Instead they discover the equivalent of an X-ray that reveals the vibrancy or the lethargy at the heart of a church, that makes visible what are otherwise invisible connections, and that offers insight into why certain patterns keep repeating themselves, either for bane or blessing.

Part 3 demonstrates how organizational intelligence significantly reshapes a particular application: succession planning and management. Every succession process involves three critical components: transition, search, and start-up. An evidence-based approach to pastoral transitions informs all three and delivers a church from the well-intentioned but often devastating effects of a one-size-fits-all methodology and into a more hopeful, customized approach. This is only one of many applications where an evidence-based discernment process using reliable organizational intelligence offers such promise.

Finally, part 4 takes up the development of organizational intelligence (OI) in churches as analogous to the development of informational technology (IT). Twenty years ago, the question "Who does your IT?" in churches drew blank looks from most leaders. Today websites, email, and social networking are integral components of the communication strategy of most congregations. A similar revolution is about to occur with OI. These chapters explain why OI is important now to a degree that it was not important previously, indeed was not possible. They also describe how leaders who systematically integrate OI into their discernment processes related to strategic planning, tactical planning, staff and board development, financial campaigns, and vocation are going to be more effective, more energized, and more fulfilled than those who do not.

At the close of every chapter, questions are posed for reflection and discussion. The concepts in this book may be unfamiliar to many and discussion with others will aid in processing new information. Leadership teams may find *Owl Sight* a useful continuing education resource. In particular, study in groups comprising both leaders and members that weigh the merits of organizational intelligence may experience particularly fruitful insights and results.

Most of us have had the experience of trying to navigate through a pitch-black room. Darkness turns every furnishing into a hazard. The corners of the table threaten bruises, the carpet edges snare the feet, and even the friendly ottoman delivers a chop block. When the light finally returns, something magical occurs. The threats are not merely removed; they are transformed into servants of our better purposes.

I am convinced that organizational intelligence can offer a transformation that is equally significant in the churches we lead and serve. If you think that is worth considering, turn the page.

Discussion Questions

1. Research indicates that those who serve in leadership positions (such as on a board or executive team, or staff members) have very different perceptions of how members are experiencing the church. Does this surprise you? Why or why not?

2. In the typical church there are those on the leadership team who believe that, overall, church members are quite positive and excited about the ministry of the church. Others on the same leadership team believe that, overall, church members are dissatisfied and uninspired. How does this affect the capacity of a leadership team to make good decisions?

3. Have you ever experienced a situation where either as a leader or as a church member, you found yourself with a perspective on how the church was doing that was very different from others around you? How did this affect you? How did you resolve the difference?

4. How would having reliable organizational intelligence on the church make your work as a leader more effective? Is there any way it might make your work as a leader more challenging?

PART 1
Foundations

CHAPTER 1

What Is Evidence-Based Discernment?

We make it harder than it has to be
And I can't tell you why
—The Eagles, "I Can't Tell You Why"

I just finished a phone conversation with a lay leader of a Presbyterian congregation who was struggling with a tough decision the leadership team had made the night before. The church has a *designated pastor*, the term for a pastor called on a two-year contract with the option for both the pastor and the congregation to extend a permanent call. After two years, the leadership had decided not to extend the call, a painful step for both people and pastor. Was it the right decision?

I pulled out a congregational assessment that they were in the process of completing. The information was compelling. Members of the congregation had become totally focused on the pastor rather than the ministries of the church, and issues regarding the work of the pastor were now near the crisis level. In the long run, this was not a fit that would work for anyone. When I shared this with him, there was an audible sigh of relief. This information from the assessments gave him the confidence to do what his intuition had been telling him all along. What he had experienced is the promise of an evidence-based discernment process.

Evidence-based discernment for ministry is a process of discovery that integrates organizational intelligence, core values, and an inspired imagination to establish a course of action. The integration of these three components produces a synergy through which each enriches and empowers the other two. Individually and in isolation, each becomes inert. We have all experienced instances of this synergy, and when we do it leaves a lasting impression. We also have experienced its absence.

Some leaders, for example, can generate both an inspired and inspiring vision for where they believe their church should go, but a failure to use organizational intelligence to clearly understand the starting point, that is, where the church is now, destines it to remain a fantasy. How many leaders today steadfastly refuse to enter into yet another planning process that will only result in another round of vision-statement T-shirts and another file in the church archives!

In other situations, leaders cling tightly to a set of core values that are so separated from organizational intelligence and an inspired imagination that they tend to degenerate into a static legalism that fosters judgmentalism and a fortress mentality. This takes many forms, but it generally can be reduced to the statement, "It doesn't matter where people are, the truth is the truth, and they need to accept that!" In many cases, organizational intelligence is the missing third strand of the braid that is needed to hold core values and an inspired imagination in a union that offers the real possibility of fruitfulness.

A Scriptural Perspective

The Scripture that best expresses this integration is Philippians 1:9–10: "And this is my prayer: that your love may abound more and more in knowledge and depth of insight, so that you may be able to discern what is best."

Love as a redemptive impulse is primary to the gospel and is irreplaceable as a motivation. Clearly, without love, our spiritual pockets are empty no matter how smart we are. But Paul sees knowledge and insight as the necessary conditions required if love is to abound. Together they form what I refer to as "smart love." Smart love is not new to any of us; we experience it most acutely in our times of need. It is what you want your lawyer, your pharmacist, and your doctor to possess. None of us would want to look up at our heart surgeon from the operating table and hear him say, "I need to tell you something. I have never actually done heart surgery before. But I do love you." We expect smart love in the people that care for us at the critical junctures of our lives. We should offer no less as Christian leaders, and we should expect no less as church members.

This integration of love (as a core value), organizational intelligence (knowledge), and an inspired imagination (insight into connections) is not simply portrayed by Paul as a promising idea or a great business principle. It is a pathway to "discerning what is best." As such, it opens the discerned course of action to divine vitalization. I, along with you, the reader, have experienced this divine activity time after time and have heard it described in a thousand ways, but no one describes it better for me than Johann Wolfgang von Goethe, who was not only a theoretical physicist but also a poet and dramatist:

> All sorts of things occur to help one that would never otherwise have occurred. A whole stream of events issues from the decision, raising in one's favor all manner of unforeseen incidents and meetings and material assistance, which no man could have dreamed would have come his way.[1]

The experience of this divine activity interlaced with the power of commitment to a well-discerned course of action provides an energy to a leadership team for which there is no substitute and which, in its state of exhaustion, the church is yearning to rediscover. Evidence-based discernment is just that: a pathway to discovering the will of God and the abundant life that permeates that discovery.

Evidence-Based Discernment and High Morale

Over time, evidence-based discernment also creates an element of mastery for leaders that is essential to generating a sustainable level of morale. Contrary to what we often believe, high morale in a leadership team is not generated by multiple "kum ba yah" experiences or pep talks but by the capacity of the team to realize significant achievements interwoven with occasions of personal and professional growth. When leaders (1) learn to integrate information with the proper spiritual motivation and a divine imagination to discern a path forward, (2) are provided with opportunities to grow and develop in their work, and (3) discover their discerned path is undergirded by the mystery of God's supporting activity, it reinforces a spiral of learning and confidence that is the antithesis of burnout and boredom.

When I was a pastor, I had a member say to me, "Ninety-three percent of the decisions you make could be made by a high school sophomore. We pay you for the other 7 percent." Most church leaders understand that they are not simply making decisions for their church that any reasonably intelligent person could make but are, rather, engaged in discernment, that is, a process for discovering what the Spirit is leading them to do next. Unraveling organizational intelligence from the discernment process is what gets leaders, as well as members, into trouble. When knowledge is separated from love, for example, it inflates the self to the diminishment of every soul within its spiritual line of sight. Paul expresses this peacockish quality in 1 Corinthians 8:1: "Knowledge puffs up, but love builds up." But the simple banishment of knowledge is no answer either. In the very same book, six chapters later, Paul writes in 1 Corinthians 14:20: "Brothers and sisters, stop thinking like children. In regard to evil be infants, but in your thinking be adults."

From a leadership perspective, it is the union of love, knowledge, and insight that gives birth to the road forward and the ability to discern what is best. It is the false dichotomy that robs the body of its neural system and abandons its leadership to a groping for reality that both frustrates and nourishes a spirit of contention. While a degree of conflict is inevitable and even healthy in any leadership team, *conflicting guesses over what is knowable is a waste of time and energy.*

Working toward this integration has been a rewarding but uphill climb. In the early days of my work with organizational intelligence, I was interviewed on a Christian radio station. I thought it went well until the end when the host of the program leaned forward, gave me his best this-is-the-most-important-question-of-the-interview look, and asked, "Some people say the church is about faith. You seem to be saying it is about numbers. How do you respond to them?" My mind went blank. Unfortunately, I kept talking. To this day I have absolutely no idea what I said!

Now that I have had about twenty years to think about it, here is what I would say: We are not about numbers. We are about listening to God's people tell their stories using symbols, and those symbols are numbers. I call a story told by numbers a *symbolic narrative.* If you have ever had pain severe enough to send you to a physician for help, you have probably experienced a symbolic narrative. At some point in the diagnosis, it is likely you were asked, "On a scale of one to ten, how bad is your pain?" The number you offer in response symbolizes your experience of pain. An "eight" speaks volumes, not only about the intensity of the pain but also about the mental energy required to cope with the pain, how incapacitating the pain is, likely causes of the pain, the urgency of treating the pain, and the measures that are likely to be effective, all from an "eight." It is a simple but powerful way to achieve an understanding of what a patient is experiencing and for a patient to feel heard.

When used in churches, a symbolic narrative helps leaders achieve an understanding of what members are *experiencing*, not simply that they are showing up. When a member is asked, "On a scale of one to six, how disturbing is the level of conflict in your church?" the member does not think "three."

Rather, the member reflects on what he or she has experienced and symbolizes it by a number. Symbolic narratives provide a way for leaders to be pastorally present to the membership *as a body* and to heed the call to be "quick to listen, slow to speak" (James 1:19) to an entire congregation, not just a few familiar voices. Christians, of all people, should be able to deal with symbols.

In my experience, the intelligence that a symbolic narrative provides to leaders is generally more reliable than the stories leaders tell themselves. I have worked with my business associate Carolyn Weese, president of Multi-Staff Ministries, for more than twenty years. We have observed a repeating pattern. We meet with church leaders who introduce themselves and their church as a "friendly church." In our first worship experience we stand in the most public place we can find, put on our best smiles, and watch hundreds of people file past us, most without a word of greeting.

If we mention this experience, leaders are, of course, incredulous. Almost invariably, after we generate the symbolic narrative ("On a scale of one to six, how friendly is this church?"), members by their own witness indicate that the church is less friendly than most in the country. Here is the choice: leaders can spend hours debating how friendly the church is. Or they can collect the organizational intelligence and save their energy for the creative, imaginative, spirit-driven process of discerning how to become more expressive of the love of God to those who walk through their doors.

Alternatives to an Evidence-Based Process

Evidence-based discernment is not an event or an episode. Rather, it is a way of approaching the entire leadership enterprise. It is to be distinguished from other processes commonly used by church leaders.

- *Impression-driven* processes tend to rely more on the internal thoughts and feelings of the people in leadership roles to gauge reality. They are characterized by statements such as "all the wisdom we need is in the room."
- *Anecdotally-driven* processes tend to rely more on conversations with individuals or groups that do not necessarily represent the entire church. These are characterized by "grapevine" information systems, which typically have choke points controlled by a few people.
- *Authority-driven* processes tend to rely more on the perspectives of those in positions of power in hierarchical systems.
- *Expert-driven* processes tend to rely more on the wisdom and knowledge resident in the mind of a highly respected and insightful individual.

Research has demonstrated that none of these four alternatives provides leaders with even a modest degree of clarity regarding the perspectives, experiences, and aspiration of members. The attitudinal patterns that drive much of a church's behavior and are decisive factors in the success or failure of a particular course of action are nearly invisible to those in leadership positions and to members as well. In some cases, the reality of a church is either counterintuitive or contradicts long-held beliefs.

In contrast to the alternatives, evidence-based discernment processes are both more public and more accountable. Impression-driven and anecdotally-driven processes rest on privately held information that is only accessible to the individual who has experienced it. Authority-driven and expert-driven processes tend to expect compliance because of the authority or expertise of one person or a small group of people. In contrast, evidence-based processes provide a depth of information that empowers *everyone* and provides an external standard against which experts can be evaluated. It is for this reason that entrenched authority-based and expert-based systems most resist an evidence-based approach.

However, it is the public element of evidence-based discernment that constitutes its power. If we are going to create healthy, vital congregations as we will define them in this book, the change cannot be accomplished by leaders alone. The entire system must shift. Every member will be required to contribute to that transformation, not as an act of obedience but as informed adults. This means that every member will need to understand why the shift is necessary and the case must be compelling enough to win their positive engagement. Neither "expert" advice nor directives from above will achieve the necessary buy-in. Evidence-based discernment is an open book generated from the perspectives, experiences, and aspirations of members themselves.

Organizational Intelligence

What information composes the organizational intelligence required for an evidence-based discernment process?

First, there is *count data*. Count data is information that can be obtained by simply counting people or things. Count data is deeply imbedded in the culture of Christian churches and in the psyche of North American Christians. Which of us born in an earlier day has not sat in a church service as children and studied the wooden hymn board firmly anchored to the wall just to the left of the chancel? The board displayed the page numbers of the hymns, a count of last Sunday's attendance, a count of the offering last Sunday, and, sometimes, a count of the offering to date. Although in many churches (but not in all), the physical hymn board has been replaced by a virtual one, the tradition of count data endures, though in digital guise. When members peruse the online denominational statistics for their church, it is the count data of membership, worship attendance, education attendance, and financial giving over a period of several years that is displayed. This is so deeply engrained in our religious culture that it does not strike us as curious that, by and large, it is the only organizational intelligence that congregations regularly collect.

What is significant about the information disclosed by count data is that it treats everything as an object. I can count how many dollars are in a pile of bills without any conversation. (If my money is speaking to me, I have larger problems.) I can count how many people are in a group without anyone speaking. Churches, however, are fundamentally enterprises of the soul, and souls can only be known as subjects who must speak to us if we are to know anything about their inner state. When the way an organization measures itself runs counter to its expressed core values, the metrics generally win. In my work, this would help explain why it has been extremely difficult to engage a significant number of local church leaders in efforts to deal with suicide and domestic violence, especially when it is emotional violence. Unless there are signs on the body such as bruises or broken bones, until there is a suicide event or self-injury that brings the issue into the objective realm, the church leader often finds it difficult to address. Yet, of all organizations, the church should be equally concerned with matters that scramble a person's emotional, spiritual, and thought life, none of which can be objectively counted.

Count data is part and parcel of a society that is authority based, mechanically modeled, and compliance focused. For our current society, which has roots in the industrial revolution, the template for our activity conforms to the pattern of assembly line production. For example, the implicit curricula of our educational system has been punctuality, dependability, and production. All these activities and systems require compliance and can be measured with some form of counting (clock, attendance record, cars produced). Similarly in the church, authority (church, Scripture, government, expert) defines how we are supposed to behave; we respond in routinized patterns (attendance, liturgy, laws, prescriptions), and the critical success factors are based upon objective criteria (numbers of people, activities, dollars, production, punctuality). While these values will never be totally replaced, they are now being *displaced* in a society that is moving toward a global culture that is more knowledge based, organically modeled, and experience focused. Knowledge (information, evidence, intelligence, know-how) influences how we think about our choices. We respond in complex, sometimes unpredictable patterns that are more like living organisms than machines (flocks, herds, schools, viruses, networks), and the critical success factors are based upon more subjective criteria (experience, energy, purpose, fulfillment).

A Wrenching Cultural Shift

This cultural shift has been wrenching not only for the church but also for many other institutional systems.

Doctors, once unquestioned authorities who could prescribe a course of action in whatever manner they chose with the expectation of punctual compliance on the part of the patient, have been forced to deal with Internet- (and pharmaceutically) educated consumers, who often have other choices for medical care in their community. They evaluate their care not based upon the basic competency of the services alone but also upon the quality of their experience, including how well they were treated. This cultural shift has not been easy, and the battles between those committed to the emerging values of patient satisfaction and safety and those characterized by the T-shirt "I am here to save your ass not kiss it" have sometimes been fierce.

While the Christian church often exhibits a tendency toward specialism and judges its suffering caused by the current culture shift unique, it is more or less following the pattern of other institutions that are slugging their way through the mire of this shift across the landscape.[2] Much has been written about this that does not need further rehearsal. Suffice it to say that the music director who responds "Over my dead body" to invitations to explore a larger variety of musical formats and the physician who responds "I don't give a rip" to patient comments that he or she is insensitive to how they are feeling are swimming in the same cultural stream. In that culture, count data works just fine.

However, another stream in which organizations are swimming takes into account more than whether people show up. I recently had surgery on my face to remove two low-level carcinomas that were close enough to one another to require a minor reconstructive procedure. As I left the office with my bandaged forehead, I was given an evaluation card that included the following questions:

Was the environment comfortable, organized?
Was the staff available to answer your questions?
What was the least positive experience on the day of your visit?
What was the most positive experience on the day of your visit?
Please rate the courtesy of the staff.

Literally thousands of organizations are shifting from simply collecting count data to also collecting what I call *witness data*.

The Vital Role of Witness Data

Witness data is information that can only be gathered when a person speaks. It treats people as subjects rather than mere objects. It assigns value not simply to showing up, paying money, or engaging in prescribed behaviors that are advantageous to the organization but also to the impact the organization is having upon the person's inner life. Witness data, it would seem, should be particularly resonant with the Christian church, given that it is led by a figure who asked, "What good is it for someone to gain the whole world, yet forfeit their soul?" (Mark 8:36).

Witness data focuses upon the PEAs: the perspectives, experiences, and aspirations of members. Member perspectives help leaders gain clarity on how people are gauging the climate of the church. Is this a place where a new person coming in can make a difference, or is the decision-making process locked up by the same small group of people? Is the church open to people from many different walks of life, or does it unintentionally cater to a relatively thin slice of the souls in the community? Does this church engage people in the practice of ministry, or does it tend toward a stadium mentality where people in the stands spend most of their time watching (and often critiquing) a few professionals on the field?

Witness data also opens a window into the quality of experience members are having in the church. Do members experience the church as a people of energy and purpose, or does it feel like they are simply going through the motions? Is their experience of the church giving new meaning to their lives, or does it leave them feeling stagnant and stuck? Does their experience of the church disturb them because conflict levels are so high, or are they developing skills to deal with conflict through mutual effort? Do they experience worship as engaging and inspiring or rote and routine?

Finally, witness data includes the aspirations of members. Nearly every person has aspirations. The word *aspiration* means literally to breathe something in. When we aspire to something, we take into ourselves a possibility that is not yet realized in our current situation. Aspirations are often the most invisible parts of the soul, because hope is always accompanied by the risk of disappointment or the sting of disapproval. It is for this reason that the aspirations of a people make up one of the most important aspects of witness data. Where do members feel that additional energy should be invested . . . or not? Is the church mining the gifts and passions of its members and shaping their ministries around those spiritual furnaces, or is it simply filling slots in the organizational structure? Do members have something to give the church but don't know how to give it? Is the church in tune with what members are trying to accomplish in their lives, or is it simply giving them more work to do?

The body of organizational intelligence generated by the answers to these questions has a profound impact upon

- the type of pastor who is a good fit for the church and likely to succeed, versus one who is a poor fit and almost certain to fail.
- the leadership tasks that must be accomplished if the church is to move forward, which, left unaddressed, will almost certainly leave the church stuck.
- the strategic plan a team develops, one that is concrete, focused, and therefore likely to be achieved versus one that is wishful, vague, and therefore likely to take its place in the file cabinet as another in a long line of forgotten plans.
- the actions that members will be asked to take, the behaviors they will encouraged to adopt, and the case they will be equipped to make with others in the church and community.

The Power of Listening

Most important of all, when leaders engage in evidence-based discernment, members feel listened to. James 1:19 urges us to be "quick to listen, slow to speak." There is good reason for this encouragement. Before we listen, the universe is only inhabited by ourselves and the projections of our own minds into other human souls. Until we listen to God, God can only be a projection of our own imagination. Only when we listen to another does that individual become a distinct person to us with an existence that transcends our own.

Taken to the scale of a church, a congregation as a whole does not have a distinct existence in the mind of a leader until that leader has engaged in a process of listening. It is easy for an entire congregation to become a projection generated by the conversations that a leader has with a relatively small circle of relationships. The disconnect, which is often not as apparent to the leader as it is to the congregation, results in a level of frustration that builds over time. In the absence of organizational intelligence, members may also develop a picture of the church that is inaccurate and become angry with others who do not see the same inaccurate picture.

In the New Testament era when churches met in homes, the relatively small scale of interpersonal relationships enabled leaders to personally listen to the entire church. The problem is that the number of dimensions in a relational network increases exponentially as people are added. If a leader has three people in the church, there are ten distinct relational patterns. When there are ten people in the church (the capacity of most living rooms), the relational patterns increase to 1,068. But when there are one hundred people in the church, the number of relational patterns increases to 1.3 x 10^{30}, more than all the grains of sand on all the beaches in the world! No wonder leaders have trouble with clarity, even in a relatively small church. Organizational intelligence (OI) offers a way to gain a better understanding of the complex systems that comprise congregations and their many parts. OI identifies important patterns that are decisive in how people feel about the church, how they deal with change, and how they will respond to their leaders. Other patterns that organizational intelligence reveals will be more fully described in chapter 10. When combined with the human experience of a listening ear, the effect can be nothing short of redemptive.

Name of Church:	*St. Thomas*
Vitality Status:	*Recovery*
Member focus:	*Pastor-focused*
Critical success factors:	*How well the pastor keeps members informed*
	How well the pastor brings out the best in everyone
Level of criticality:	*Urgent*
Organizational culture:	*Hearth and Home*

Figure 1.1. St. Thomas Church Organizational Intelligence Profile.
For a definition of terms, please see the glossary in appendix A.

We have all discovered how powerfully healing it can be when someone simply listens to us. The same is true for an entire church, and the impact can be lasting. Several years ago, I led a church through a process of evidence-based discernment. The organizational intelligence for St. Thomas is found in figure 1.1. (Note: A fuller discussion of the components that make up an organizational intelligence profile for a congregation begins with chapter 5. A full set of organizational intelligence for a congregation consists of several substantial documents that require hours to read and digest. For the purposes of this book, a radically abbreviated form of organizational intelligence is represented in figures titled "Organizational Intelligence Profile." For those readers who want to wade into a more thorough representation of organizational intelligence, please go to www.holycowconsulting.com/owlsight/sample.htm.)

Sometime later I received the following letter:

Dear Russ,
I thought I'd take a moment to let you know how things are going at St. Thomas. An unexpected and significant change took place in the parish after you made your report. The tension in the parish almost disappeared. This unexplained reduction in the expressed level of conflict was experienced by a wide variety

of people. I was dubious at first. You may remember that I mentioned this situation to you when you visited us the second time.

Well . . . we are continuing to experience good things. Parishioners are taking on more responsibility for key ministries and are making headway in the process to reorient the parish to be outwardly focused. We lost a couple of people who were most conflicted, and we are gaining new people. The face of the congregation is changing.

The diminished level of conflict has made it easier for me to function and has freed up those who were feeling good to do more of what they wanted to do. No doubt, we will face the typical conflicts that parishes face in the future. However, it seems that we have been delivered from the nasty effects of the conflict that sought to tear us apart. I wanted to thank you again for sharing your ministry with us.

Peace,
Pastor Pete

Your church may resemble this description of St. Thomas Church, or it might be quite different. Whatever the situation, when members feel they have been heard accurately, the chances of developing a healthier congregation increase dramatically. How many times I have spent a couple hours unfolding the story provided by organizational intelligence (and sometimes some very difficult information) to have folks seek me out afterwards and say with an appreciate wonder, "You know who we are and you have never even met us before!" If you are a leader or member of a church, you could probably give a fairly accurate count of the number of people who worship there. But do you really know the perspectives, experiences, and aspirations that are residing inside those bodies in the pews? Remember, we are talking about the collective witness of the entire church, which may be quite different from those in your immediate circle. If you want to take a shot at estimating the PEAs (perspectives, experiences, and aspirations) of the members of your church, go to www.holycowconsulting.com/owlsight/leadershipclarity.htm and take the *Leadership Clarity Check®*.

If leaders simply had a better read on the perspectives, experiences, and aspirations of their members, that alone would be revolutionary. However, it is important to recognize that the journey into evidence-based discernment, like any journey into greater self-awareness, requires preparation. In order to benefit from an evidence-based approach, leaders must be ready to

- trust the instruments that are used to generate organizational intelligence and not revert to the dangerous practice of flying by the seat of their pants.
- accept the surprises that are revealed through organizational intelligence, even if they call long-standing assumptions into question.

- deal with the spiritual challenges of organizational intelligence and employ the resources of the gospel.

These are the subjects of the next three chapters, which will lay the foundation for an evidence-based approach to church leadership and membership.

Discussion Questions

1. Philippians 1:9–10 suggests that a process that helps us discern what is best for Christian communities weaves together love and knowledge. I refer to this as "smart love." In your experience of the church, either as a member or a leader, do you feel that there has been a need for more love (positive motivation) or more knowledge (reliable and useful information)?

2. The chapter asserts that three elements are required to create a high-functioning leadership team:
   - Processes that integrate information with the proper spiritual motivation and a divine imagination to discern a path forward
   - Opportunities for members to grow and develop in their work
   - Experiences in which leaders discover their discerned path is undergirded by the mystery of God's supporting activity, reinforcing a spiral of learning and confidence that is the antithesis of burnout and boredom

   How or when has your leadership experience in the church reflected those three elements?

3. What are some of the examples of count data in your church that are used in leadership decisions? What are some examples of witness data? Is there good balance between the two in the congregation? How does the balance or imbalance affect the way that congregational decisions are made?

CHAPTER 2

Preparing for the Journey: Trusting the Instruments

Things are seldom what they seem,
Skim milk masquerades as cream;
Highlows pass as patent leathers;
Jackdaws strut in peacock's feathers.

Very true,
So they do.

—Gilbert and Sullivan, "Things Are Seldom What They Seem," *HMS Pinafore*

O n the evening of July 16, 1999, a Piper Saratoga took off from the Essex County Airport in New Jersey. After departure, the aircraft reached a cruising altitude of 5,500 feet and flew along the Connecticut shoreline until turning directly toward Martha's Vineyard. At 9:33 p.m., while over water about 34 miles west of Martha's Vineyard, the aircraft began a descent. Radar data showed the descent rate initially varied from 400 to 600 feet per minute. At about 9:38 p.m., the aircraft began a bank in a right-wing-down direction. Thirty seconds later, the descent stopped at 2,200 feet and the aircraft began a climb that lasted another 30 seconds, stopping at 2,500 feet with wings level by 9:39 p.m. Less than a minute later, the plane entered a left climbing turn to 2,600 feet, and then began a descent that reached a rate of about 900 feet per minute. At 9:40 p.m. the wings were leveled.

Eight seconds later, the plane banked in a right-wing-down direction and the bank angle, descent rate, and airspeed began to increase, with the descent reaching as high as 4,700 feet per minute. The plane crashed into the ocean about 9:41 p.m.. Pilots flying in the vicinity at the time of the accident reported that no visible horizon existed over the water. Spatial disorientation was ruled the most likely cause of the accident.

This is the account of the last eight minutes of the life of John F. Kennedy Jr., his wife, Carolyn Bessette Kennedy, and his sister-in-law, Lauren Bessette. They died as the result of spatial disorientation, one of general aviation's biggest killers.

Spatial disorientation occurs when a pilot loses sight of the horizon or some other external visual reference. In the absence of that critical piece of external information, the pilot has a choice. On the one hand, the pilot can choose to trust his instruments for guidance. Alternatively, the pilot can choose to trust his or her own internal sense of up, down, right, and left. A pilot can believe that he is as level as he would be if seated at his dining room table when the plane is actually banked to the right and in a graveyard spiral, hurtling toward the earth. This "flying by the seat of the pants" is the number one cause of aircraft deaths.

The human brain did not develop the capacity to accurately perceive spatial reality while moving at hundreds of miles per hour in three-dimensional space. As neurologist Andrew Newberg points out in the book *How God Changes Your Brain,*

> Having an accurate perception of reality is not one of the brain's strong points. The human brain seems to have difficulty separating fantasies from facts. It sees things that are not there, and it sometimes doesn't see things that are there. In fact, the brain doesn't even try to create a fully detailed map of the external world.[1]

When we fail to adopt a means of perceiving that is scaled to reality, reality will shift to the scale of our perceptions. If we try to fly a plane using our sensory impressions without having a visual horizon, the plane will eventually slow down to the scale of our perceptual capacity. A crash is an instant adjustment of reality to the scale of our perceptual capacity.

Similarly, the human brain did not develop the capacity to accurately read the perceptions of a large network of people. Human beings have learned to survive by sustaining a small network of interdependent relationships, typically a family or a clan. We tend to forget that the New Testament church began as house churches. Think about how many folks you can squeeze into your living room and you have an estimate of the size of the original church. You also have an estimate of the size of a group that members can accurately "read" through our own inner impressions. Jesus had twelve disciples whom he could read fairly well, but beyond that he had to augment his impressions with a more formal process of inquiry. "[Jesus] asked them, 'Who do people say I am?'" (Mark 8:27).

As a human being, Jesus knew his limits, but leaders who have been shaped by a religious culture that is almost totally impression-driven can find it difficult to focus on the instruments provided by an evidence-based discernment process. As a result, the size and complexity of the church drops to the scale of the leaders' perceptual capacities, sometimes sharply. It is the church equivalent of a plane crash. What follows is a typical example.

When a Church Fails to Trust Its Instruments

First Congregational Church is one of the largest churches in the Midwest. It grew under the leadership of a gifted pastor who served the church for a dozen years and then left in 2005 to start a nonprofit organization serving inner-city children. After he left, the church engaged in an evidence-based discernment process that involved collecting a reliable set of organizational intelligence from the church members. The church scored high energy, high satisfaction. However, the process also revealed that one of the most critical factors affecting how people felt about the church was the degree of tolerance for differences of opinion. (See figure 2.1.) The level of criticality was high, which means that increasing the level of tolerance was a very important task for the leadership to focus on.

Name of Church:	*First Congregational*
Vitality Status:	*Transformational*
Member focus:	*Ministry-focused*
Critical success factors:	*Level of tolerance for differing opinions*
Level of criticality:	*High*
Organizational culture:	*Performance*

Figure 2.1. First Congregational Church Organizational Intelligence Profile, Initial Assessment. For a definition of terms, please see the glossary in appendix A.

Many churches like First Congregational that are theologically very conservative are also organizationally brittle. While they may be thriving at any particular point in their life cycle, a significant issue on which members disagree can shatter the church and catapult it into a steep decline. The evidence suggests that it is critical for these churches to learn some conflict management skills and increase their level of tolerance in order to develop some "bounce, not break" capacity. If they wait until they are in the middle of the fall, it is often too late.

When the leaders of First Congregational were presented with this information, they did what many more conservative churches do: asserted that tolerance was a liberal value that they did not share. They also indicated that a conservative, less tolerant theology was key to their success and they didn't want to risk that. However, as the next chapter will discuss, the evidence indicates that a particular theological perspective is not a factor in church vitality, but leaders tend to trust their impressions more than the evidence. They ignored the finding and moved on to other findings that were more in line with their intuitions.

The church then proceeded to search for and call a pastor whose abilities and motivations were totally at odds with the organizational intelligence they had collected. There were a number of reasons for this, but they boil down to a regression to internal impressions that were politically imposed upon the system. In times of stress people tend to go backwards, regressing to childlike behavior; they have difficulty perceiving that others are different and experience the world in their own distinct ways.

Under the stress of the transition process, several members of the search committee stopped attending to the organizational intelligence in hand that gave evidence of a congregation independent of their own internal impressions. In particular, one longtime, influential member adopted the position that he would oppose anyone who did not meet his internal criteria regardless of the organizational intelligence coming from the congregation. Since the search committee had adopted a principle that any candidate would need a unanimous vote from the search committee, one member held veto power over the entire process. A pastor was finally called. Members reacted in predictable fashion with some favoring the new pastor, others not. Because the church had not developed the capacity to exercise tolerance in the face of differences, a sharp conflict quickly ensued. Members withheld money—a power solution to the conflict—which created a major crisis for the church. Staff members were let go, programs were cut, and payments to creditors were delayed. The new pastor was gone within a year.

By the time the church ran another round of data gathering, the church had plummeted from one of the most vibrant congregations in the region to one of the more troubled ones. Every metric of church health had dropped. The average age of the church increased as many young people drifted away. As younger people left, the church lost some of its dynamism with a corresponding loss in flexibility. Giving as a percentage of household income had fallen from an incredible 4 percent to only 1.4 percent. One thing that has not changed at First Congregational is that increasing tolerance is still a critical success factor, but now it has been joined by disturbing levels of conflict and a concern that leaders do not represent the congregation. (See figure 2.2.)

Name of Church:	*First Congregational*
Vitality Status:	*Recovery*
Critical success factors:	*Level of tolerance for differing opinions*
	Leader responsiveness to member concerns
Level of criticality:	*High*
Priority Focus:	*Hearth and home*

Figure 2.2. First Congregational Church Organizational Intelligence Profile, Follow-up Assessment. For a definition of terms, please see the glossary in appendix A.

What First Congregational has experienced are the consequences of defaulting to an impression-driven discernment process, even when the evidence was suggesting a very different course. By failing to focus on the critical factors that came out of their own listening process, they triggered a cascade of events that spun the church into free fall. This story illustrates how disciplined leaders must be to make the shift to an evidence-based discernment process and to actually focus on what they have learned.

It Can Be Done

When church leaders are offered the possibility of a different way of discerning a path forward, I sometimes hear that it can't be done, either because it is too difficult or because they do not think it will work. The truth is that it can be done because it is being done.

Name of Church:	*Presbytery of Greater Atlanta*
Vitality Status:	*Recovery/chaos*
Critical success factors:	*Meaningful meetings, shared vision*
Level of criticality:	*High*
Priority Focus:	*Congregational vitality*

Figure 2.3. Presbytery of Greater Atlanta Organizational Intelligence Profile

Contrast the story above with the experience of the Presbytery of Greater Atlanta. In response to a projected budget shortfall, they entered into an evidence-based process to discern what to do. They discovered that less than 30 percent of respondents were clearly satisfied with the presbytery overall. When they drilled down into the data they discovered that one critical success factor for improving how session members felt about the presbytery was to improve how members experienced presbytery meetings. Only 22 percent of respondents clearly agreed that presbytery meetings were a good use of their time and energy. (See figure 2.3.)

Dr. Thomas Evans, the new presbytery executive, took that information seriously. He instituted a number of changes in how meetings were conducted. Then he began to track how members were experiencing those meetings by surveying attendees. He began his tracking in November 2010. By May 2011 he had seen a significant improvement. The May results are shown in figure 2.4.

I felt this was a fantastic meeting	*19%*
I felt this was a good meeting	*74%*
I did not feel this was a good meeting	*3%*
I felt this was a terrible meeting	*3%*

Figure 2.4. Tracking a Critical Success Factor—Meaningful Meetings

The presbytery made major changes in a number of other areas in response to the organizational intelligence they collected. While the evidence on the overall impact of these changes is yet to be collected, early indications are positive, including an increase in financial giving to the presbytery.

Making these changes is hard work, but it is easier to sustain when there is real evidence that supports it.

What Makes the Difference?

What are the differences between churches that are able to benefit from organizational intelligence and those that are not? Here are the critical factors I have observed:

- A leader at the helm (pastor, executive, bishop) who *invests* time and energy in understanding organizational intelligence and is *committed* to turning it into action
- A leader at the helm (pastor, executive, bishop) who is *secure* enough to handle evaluative information without becoming defensive or discouraged
- A leadership team that is willing to accept information that is a *corrective* to their own impressions and anecdotal data

- A leadership team that has *realistic expectations* about organizational information, recognizing that it provides not answers but clarity about the starting point
- A leadership team that uses organizational intelligence to *inform* their leadership but not as an excuse for abdicating leadership
- A leadership team that is able to weave together organizational intelligence with other important *sources of creativity*, including best practices, imagination, and spiritual practice
- A leadership team that is *strong enough to resist* the efforts of those who exert personal or political pressure to return to processes that ignore the organizational intelligence
- A leadership team that is committed to *tracking progress* over time on key measurements
- A congregation that is open to growing in its own self-awareness, both its strengths and its shadows
- A congregation that is able to accept and deal with its own spiritual dissonance
- For a list of assessment instruments that generate organizational intelligence, see appendix B: Tools.

This chapter touched on a fact that many find surprising: A low level of tolerance tends to create churches that are conflicted and demoralized instead of producing a church where members hold a common theological perspective that unifies and galvanizes. A number of surprises such as these emerge when we engage in an evidence-based discernment process. Preparing for these surprises is the subject of the next chapter.

Discussion Questions

1. This chapter begins by comparing the experience of church leadership and not being clear about where the church is with the experience of piloting a plane and not always being able to see the horizon. How are these experiences the same? How are they different?

2. Andrew Newberg writes that "having an accurate perception of reality is not one of the brain's strong points." How does this make leadership more challenging?

3. First Congregational Church had good organizational intelligence on the church as a system, but leaders chose instead to navigate based upon their own impressions. As I stated above, they failed to trust their instruments. Compared to people in other important endeavors, do

you think church leaders have a harder time trusting information (for example, doctors trusting X-rays, pilots trusting instruments, juries trusting evidence in a trial)?

4. The Presbytery of Greater Atlanta responded to their organizational intelligence in a very different manner. Without knowing much about them, what do you think might have made the difference?

CHAPTER 3

Preparing for the Journey: Admitting Surprises

The real voyage of discovery consists not in seeking new landscapes, but in having new eyes.

—Marcel Proust, French author, 1871–1922

In July of 1980, the Hyatt Regency in Kansas City opened to the public after four years of design and construction. It was an impressive sight. This hotel consisted of a forty-story hotel tower and conference facilities, which were connected by an open concept atrium. Inside the atrium were three walkways that connected the hotel to the conference facilities on the second, third, and fourth floors. The atrium was 145 feet long, 117 feet wide, and 50 feet high.

Originally, the second and fourth floor walkways were to be suspended from the same hanger rod and held in place by a single nut. For several reasons, the design was changed to add a second hanger rod secured with a second nut. To the eye, it appears that this would actually double the strength of the support. The engineer signed off on the redesign without checking it.

On the evening of July 17, 1981, between 1,500 and 2,000 people inundated the atrium floor and the suspended walkways to see a local radio station's dance competition. At 7:05 p.m., a loud crack echoed throughout the building and the second and fourth floor walkways crashed to the ground, killing 114 people and injuring more than 200 others. It was the worst structural failure in the history of the United States.

A subsequent review of the cause of the disaster revealed that while it seemed that the addition of a second hanging rod and nut would strengthen the support of the walkway, *it actually doubled the load that the nut had to support*. The evidence did not support an assumption that was critical to the entire design.

The Unthinkable: What If Our Ministries Are Built on False Assumptions?

The ministries of Christian churches are also designed around assumptions that, on the face of it, seem intuitively obvious. Whatever one might think of Willow Creek and seeker service megachurches, I have to respect founder Bill Hybels for moving to an evidence-based discernment process. Many people think of megachurch leaders like Hybels as simply investing megaresources in communication or even entertainment. In fact, he has invested more resources than the average congregation in using technology to listen to the witness of his members. From that listening process Hybels came to the conclusion that several of the fundamental assumptions on which his entire ministry was based were not true. Speaking at the Leadership Summit, Hybels summarized the findings this way:

> Some of the stuff that we have put millions of dollars into[,] thinking it would really help our people grow and develop spiritually, when the data actually came back, it wasn't helping people that much. Other things that we didn't put that much money into and didn't put much staff against is stuff our people are crying out for.[1]

Having spent thirty years creating and promoting a multimillion dollar organization driven by programs and measuring participation, and convincing other church leaders to do the same, you can see why Hybels called this research "the wake-up call" of his adult life.

Dealing with the Counterintuitive

As Christians, we, above all others, should be open to embracing that which is not intuitively obvious. The concept of Trinity, God in fellowship with God, probably comes near the top of the list. As a person with a degree in physics, I have learned that much of what we now know about the universe is counterintuitive. In fact, the technology that powers your cell phone, computer, television, GPS, and nearly every appliance in your home is built upon the assumption that some things can simultaneously be in two places at the same time.

In both the religious world and the scientific world, important discoveries are made by those who are willing to look at the actual evidence with an open mind. If we are going to benefit from evidence-based discernment, we must be willing to be surprised. Let's look at some examples.

Surprise 1: Leaders Do Not Have Clarity Regarding the Perspectives, Experiences, and Aspirations of Church Members

The fact that leaders lack clarity about members' perceptions was already established in the introduction to the book. But what was not addressed is that leaders are surprised to discover this lack of clarity because they are operating under the assumption that everyone is seeing the same church. Please note I am not saying that leaders would be surprised to discover that they disagree with other leaders occasionally on what the church should do. Disagreement is a monthly (and healthy) reality. What surprises them is to discover that different leaders are perceiving two or three substantially different churches. This double- or triple-vision makes it extremely difficult for a leadership team to navigate the tempestuous seas of today's church. Nonetheless, it feels normal, because it is all they have ever known.

The same can be said regarding the perceptions that members have of fellow members. It would surprise most members to discover how little clarity they have regarding the perspectives, experiences, and aspirations of the membership as a whole.

This would not be so problematic if it were not linked to a second assumption, namely, that the critical factor for the renewal of churches is the discovery and application of a standard set of programs, policies, and procedures. While we have become quite adept at understanding size dynamics in churches, we have a meager understanding of other aspects of organizational intelligence. As a consultant, I am fortunate enough to overhear a robust, wide-ranging conversation among pastors, denominational leaders, program developers, and consultants of all kinds (strategic, succession, transition, and financial). What strikes me about the conversation is that much of it occurs without probing the starting point, which includes the vitality status, the member focus, and the organizational culture of the congregation or staff under discussion. Most leaders are surprised to learn not only that they lack clarity as a team regarding the current state of the church; they also have never considered the fact that different organizational cultures, for example, require different strategies, with different leadership styles, and different developmental tasks in order to be effective. This is the first surprise of organizational intelligence.

Surprise 2: Member Spiritual Vitality and Church Vitality

In the next chapter I will address the importance of understanding an evidence-based discernment process as a spiritual journey for the congregation. But what about the individual spiritual journey? What impact does individual spiritual practice have on the vitality of the church as a whole?

When members bear witness to this personal aspect of their spiritual practice, they speak of a variety of spiritual experiences that affect how they view life. They may speak of different ways in which they experience the presence of God in their lives or their efforts to extend the impact of their faith into the whole of their lives, family life, work life, friendships, and so forth. Some may give expression to a deep commitment to put God first in their lives. Given the fact that we are dealing with churches and the churches' proclamation that a deeper relationship with God improves the quality of our life with one another, one would expect that as members' spiritual vitality increases, the positive energy level in the church would also increase. The graph in figure 3.1 represents what we would expect to see: the higher the individual spiritual vitality, the higher the energy in the congregation.

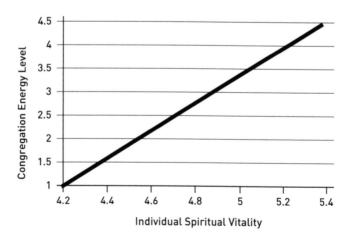

Figure 3.1. What We Expect

What we discover when we look at the actual evidence is illustrated in figure 3.2. It is nearly a random pattern. Some churches where members bear witness to lower levels of individual spiritual vitality actually have higher energy levels, and vice versa. In fact, individual spiritual vitality contributes only about 4 percent to a congregation's energy level!

I have led planning sessions where I have introduced that single piece of information and watched it temporarily lock up the meeting. Many of us have heard for so many years, and some of us (including myself) have preached and taught, that if we just get our individual relationships right with God, everything else in the church will take care of itself. We find it inconceivable that it might be false. The lack of evidence for a relationship between individual spiritual vitality and the energy level of a congregation suggests two things in a discernment process.

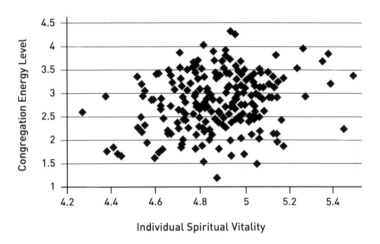

Figure 3.2. What We Actually See

First, efforts to deepen the individual spiritual lives of members do not necessarily lead to an energized, purposeful, joyful, welcoming, healing, supportive, learning, or engaged congregation. This is not to say that individual spiritual formation is unimportant. It is saying that individual spiritual formation, isolated from the experience of *corporate* spiritual formation and lacking in the living connections between spirituality and how we live with one another, is not a path that the broader church has found fruitful for increasing the health and vitality of a congregation. Developing health and vitality in a congregation requires something more.

Second, the converse is also true. We cannot assume that a church that is energized, purposeful, joyful, welcoming, healing, supportive, learning, and engaged will necessarily lead to individuals who are growing in their own personal spiritual lives. As Hybels discovered, getting members more and more involved in a "hopping" church does little to develop their spiritual lives. Again, this is not to say that developing vital congregations is unimportant. Something more is needed for individual spiritual formation.

Once a leadership team accepts this reality, when the familiar way forward is blocked, it can begin the spiritual journey of creatively and prayerfully exploring the question, What corporate spiritual practices might lead to healthy, vital churches? Is there a different way of being together in prayer, for example, that creates a spiritual field into which people walk and are healed before anyone says a word to them?

The other side of the coin must also be explored. How do churches that are healthy and vital make sure that their members are growing spiritually? For example, do we need to be offering opportunities for spiritual formation such as spiritual direction, mentoring, retreats, and pilgrimages in churches where the tendency is to assume that spirituality is a personal matter that we should leave to individual initiative?

The Promise of Evidence-Based Discernment: A New Set of Questions

One of the promises of an evidence-based discernment process is that it poses a new set of questions. In some cases, it blocks the familiar path forward so that a deeper spiritual creativity can be engaged. It invites us to stop casting and retrieving our empty nets on the same side of the boat. In response to criticism that his work on an electric light was producing no results, Thomas Edison is reported to have said, "Results! Why, man, I have gotten a lot of results. I know several thousand things that won't work." A no answer is also an answer. It invites us to keep looking in new directions.

Surprise 3: The Bible and Church Vitality

Before we leave the topic of surprises, I would like to wrestle one other myth to the ground. It has to do with the Bible. When Christians bear witness to their understanding of the Bible in various churches across the country, they exhibit a wide range of views. In some churches, more than 90 percent of the members would speak about the Bible as a book that is without error of any sort: historical, scientific, cosmological, or geographical. In other churches more than 90 percent of the members would take a completely different view and affirm that while the Bible is inspired and is a reliable revelation of God and God's ultimate purposes, it was never intended to be a science or history textbook.

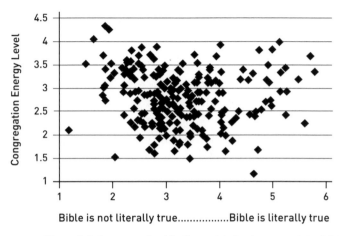

Figure 3.3. Congregation Vitality and Attitudes toward the Bible

Not only do people hold these widely divergent points of view, they also often believe that converting other people in the church to their particular perspective on the Bible is paramount to recovering a higher level of health and vitality in their congregation. I have had a number of conversations with members on the more conservative side who are concerned about the health of their church. They take me aside and express the view that if members would return to a literal interpretation of the Bible, God would once again bless their church. If they are right, then we would expect to see a pattern across hundreds of churches where congregations that hold this more literal perspective on the Scripture would also have a greater sense of energy, purpose, enthusiasm, and engagement.

Folks on the more progressive side of the church can be similarly enthusiastic about conversions in the opposite direction. Armed with hope that freeing people from a literalistic interpretation of the Bible will usher in a more tolerant, relevant, and therefore energized church, they tend toward a more issue-centered approach to ministry. There is the implicit promise that if Christians had a better understanding of the historical context and limitations of the Scripture, they would create churches that were less dogmatic, more loving, and more constructively engaged with the world. If they are right, then we would expect to see a pattern across hundreds of churches where congregations that hold this less literal perspective on the Scripture would also have a greater sense of energy, purpose, enthusiasm, and engagement.

In fact we see neither. (See figure 3.3.) When we examine the energy level in congregations in order to discover a relationship to the view they hold of the Bible, we find that one does not exist. The path to a high-energy church could be through a more conservative theology . . . or a more liberal one. A particular theological perspective contributes less than 1 percent to the energy level of a congregation. If we split all the denominations in the United States into conservative and progressive branches, we will have the same number of dispirited congregations spread among twice as many denominations. Because theological perspective is not a reliable predictor of congregational vitality, we can assume that any division of congregations by theological perspective will yield the same percentage of low morale churches in each of them. Assume we have twenty churches in a denomination and half of them are dispirited. That's ten. If we split the denomination into two by theological perspective with half liberal and half conservative, it is likely that each will have five dispirited congregations. We haven't created a stronger denomination in the process. We have merely created two denominations with the same vulnerabilities. Therefore theological purity, of whatever brand, will not solve the problems faced by most churches in the United States.

The Importance of Experience

There was a time in U.S. history when religious engagement was normative for people living here. Relatively little energy needed to be invested in concern for the quality of experience members were finding in the churches they attended. Leaders and members alike had the luxury of investing large amounts of time and energy in defining (and debating) a particular theological position over against another. That time is gone. In the typical Christian church, more than a third of the members agree, that to one degree or another, they are simply going through the motions of church activity regardless of theological perspective. Neither doctrinal statements nor position papers will repair that.

Again, this is not to say that theology is unimportant. Theology is the engine that drives the entire Christian enterprise. However, the engine of a car and the wheels are independent critical systems. My father had a mechanical mind and vocation. He often viewed life through that lens. Whenever people were so focused on solving one part of a problem that they were ignoring another critical aspect, he would say, "The wheels came off." If we put all our energy into tuning the engine and pay no attention to the fact that the wheels are coming off, the car is going nowhere. The religious landscape is now littered with the bodies of rusted-out churches that invested all their energy into one theological battle or another, one current issue or another, while ignoring the what people experienced when they walked into their buildings.

At this point it may seem that evidence-based processes only throw up dead-end signs. Of course, a dead-end sign also is a gift. It keeps you from having to journey all the way down a road to discover that it doesn't lead anywhere. An evidence-based process puts up dead-end signs on many of the failure paths that are a waste of time and energy. That alone would be useful. Even better are the signs indicating you are on the *right* road. Evidence-based processes offer those as well.

Surprise 4: The Six Things a Church Must Do Well . . . No Matter What

In my work as a consultant I have found that the members of high-energy congregations consistently bear witness to the following six characteristics of their churches:[2]

> Vital worship
> Lifelong learning
> Spiritual formation that fits complex lifestyles
> An open leadership system
> Quality relationships
> Flexibility

Figure 3.4 reveals just how well these factors predict the vitality of a church and would suggest that these are the areas where leaders and members need to be investing a significant amount of their time and energy if they want to experience a renewal of their churches.

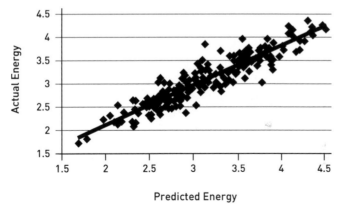

Figure 3.4. Six Factor Fit.

For me, this is another surprise. Given all the different churches, their varying sizes, settings, styles, and social characteristics, the same six factors predict their level of vitality. Here are the two caveats:

- How the factors are developed varies depending upon the starting point. Since effective churches tend to build on strengths, the factors that are developed first will vary from church to church depending upon the assets they begin with.
- Most church leaders (and members) have not had enough training to know how to develop a church where an overwhelming number of members would affirm that the church is doing a great job in those six areas.

What Leaders Tend to Do Well: The Administrative Function

Most church leaders are trained to excel at the administrative function of the organization, which is the collection of activities that the church engages in to manage its internal operations.

The administrative function is *focused* on maintenance issues.

It *values* doing the thing *right*.

It is *aimed* at addressing the needs of people on the inside.

It is important for *short-term efficiency* (one to three years)

Some examples of the administrative function include the following:

- How to use Robert's Rules of Order
- A working knowledge of the church constitution, canons, and bylaws
- Creating policies and procedures to guide the church operationally
- Renewing articles of incorporation
- Dealing with tax and liability issues
- Creating and approving a budget
- Knowing how to read a financial statement
- Electing officers and appointing people to various roles
- Managing and maintaining facilities
- Setting expectations for and managing personnel
- Establishing times for worship and education
- Establishing standards and exercising discipline
- Settling disputes through a majority vote

I did not appreciate how masterful the church is at dealing with these critical functions until I started a project for abandoned children with HIV in Honduras. Having to establish all these administrative functions for a new nonprofit organization from scratch is a surprisingly daunting task. Yet most church leaders handle them as a matter of course. When confronted with the challenge of creating a vital church, most leaders will default to what they do best: administer.

What Is Critical for Leaders to Do Well: The Performance Function

What leaders are not trained to do is to address the performance function of a church, which is the collection of activities it currently engages in to fulfill its mission and achieve the vision.

The performance function is *focused* on fruitfulness.

It *values* doing the *right* thing.

It is *aimed* at addressing the needs of people on the inside *and* the outside.

It is important for *short-term effectiveness* (one to three years)

Every leadership team needs to allocate a significant portion of its time and energy to addressing performance issues, such as the six factors mentioned earlier. However, it is my experience that church leaders at every level tend to retain administrative functions and delegate performance functions. The result is a church with a fragmented, unaligned, and siloed collection of ministries overseen by a superb administrative board, which is perplexed that, despite its best efforts, the church continues to decline.

Unfortunately, poor administration in a church is a dissatisfier, but great administration alone does not make for a vital church. A *dissatisfier* is something that can ruin an enterprise if it is not accomplished, but addressing a dissatisfier does not make an enterprise successful in and of itself. Not changing the oil in your car can make for a lousy vacation (when the engine blows up), but a great vacation requires more than having a well-serviced car. This is the final surprise for many church leaders, that something beyond good administrative function might be required of them.

I read a book by a therapist a few months ago. He said something that I had never really thought about before. He wrote, "I assume that when I make a suggestion to a person for the very first time, he or she is going to resist it. So I wait for the initial resistance to subside. Then I bring it up again." Given that organizational intelligence, as described in this book, is relatively new and that some of the surprises are quite . . . surprising, we should expect some level of resistance. We should also be prepared for folks to revert to familiar patterns, even when those patterns are not proving fruitful. In the next chapter, we will examine the final and most important preparation for an evidence-based discernment process: the spiritual journey.

Discussion Questions

1. This chapter recounts how a basic assumption (two bolts are better than one) ended up being the cause of the collapse of the walkway in the Hyatt Regency Hotel. List the three or four basic assumptions (not doctrinal or theological) on which the ministry of your church is built. For example, that getting people to come to church will positively affect their lives.

2. Through organizational intelligence, Bill Hybels realized that several key assumptions of his entire ministry were not true. What would you do if you realized that one or more of the assumptions listed in the question above were discovered not to be true?

3. Many of us as leaders have preached and taught that if members just get their personal relationship with God in the right place, everything else will take care of itself. The research indicates that this is not true: churches where members bear witness to very vibrant personal relationships with God are often beset by low morale, waves of conflict, and a lack of care for one another. How might this change your view of the best way to build a strong church?

CHAPTER 4

Preparing for the Journey: The Unlived Life

At first you go into yourself and there is nothing.
Then you go a little deeper, and there is something.
—Rami Kalfon, "Excerpts from *The Reality Of Being*," in *Parabola* 34, no. 4

I work with about a hundred churches every year helping them acquire the organizational intelligence necessary for an evidence-based discernment process. Most of the emails and phone calls I receive are questions about how to prepare a congregation for the mechanics of an assessment process. In twenty-five years of doing this work, I have never received a request for resources to equip leaders and members for the spiritual labor required in taking a deep look in the mirror, which is an essential foundation in a process of collecting organizational intelligence.

It could be that they have developed their own resources or that they are relying on their current spiritual practice to steady and ground them for their work. More likely they have not had enough experience with evidence-based discernment to know that its fruit is born out of an invisible spiritual practice that nourishes the faith and courage on which all depends. Research shows that about half of all people quit psychotherapy prematurely. Without the benefit of research, I would estimate that roughly the same percentage of church leaders quit the assessment process prematurely and revert to pathways that, while more familiar, will not lead anywhere new. For many leadership teams, spiritual practice has been reduced to bookend prayers rather than a protein that permeates the work. For that reason, you may be tempted to skip this chapter. I implore you not to do that.

Something More

The first area requiring spiritual preparation is developing an openness to the unlived life. In addition to the well-explored and familiar life that they live on a daily basis, churches carry within their corporate souls an unlived life. It is a life that resides in the shadows, just beneath the surface of the routine, but it is sensed well enough as an alternative to the status quo that it results in a vague and chronic dissatisfaction. At high tide, the urgent matters at hand flood the system, leaving a predictable surface of ripple and wave with the occasional whitecaps of conflict. Only at low tide, when the press of the urgent recedes, is there sometimes a glimpse of structures not typically observed, the landscape and contours of another life that is possible but not embraced.

This unlived life beckons powerfully and insistently. Ignoring the call of God found in it often leaves us with an unanswerable sense of regret. At the individual level, this unlived life was characterized by the words of a terminally ill patient who responded to a well-meaning chaplain, "You don't understand, chaplain. I am not crying because I am dying. I am crying because I never lived."[1]

Churches, many now on the verge of collapse, do not lend themselves to this kind of compact, personal dialogue. But their symbolic narratives using digital assessments tell the same story as the patient quoted above. Typically, roughly a third of those responding to a standard assessment instrument indicate, to one degree or another, they are simply going through the motions. In some churches it is as high as two-thirds. It is a sobering fact that most Christians living today have *never* experienced a church driven by a universal perception of energy and purpose among the members. The yearly accumulation of this motion without meaning, layer upon layer, can only be disquieting, because in the shadows is another life that, though invisible and unlived, stands in contrast and is believed to be possible.

Jesus and the Unlived Life

The lived life of the carpenter Jesus of Nazareth held the unlived life of the Messiah. The Christian message hangs on the journey of Jesus from one life into the other and offers us the hopeful pattern for the journeys into our own unlived lives should we choose them. He begins by opening his soul to fresh voices that can speak to the other life that he intuits is there. If he stays in the carpentry shop where he absorbs the same daily stream of messages focused on materials, construction orders, and the praises or problems of customers, he will be held fast in the inescapable web of his same life.

Jesus finds the new voices at the Jordan River; in a change of setting and amid the sensual inputs of sight, sound, and touch that open the spirit; in the urgent, distinctive tones of John the Baptist and the mysterious but compelling message, "You are my Son, whom I love; with him I am well pleased" (Matt. 3:17). Now Jesus does something so remarkable that it almost escapes our notice. He gives more weight to the voice of this experience than he gives to the sum total of all the other voices in his previous thirty years of life. If he does not find a way to quell the volume of those past affirmations and admonitions, whatever their authority or strength, he will be bound to the life he already knows. To discover his unlived life, he must make himself vulnerable to the new voices calling his name.

To discover their unlived lives, churches also must extend their capacity to hear other voices sounding in the world. A few of these voices may come from some distance, from other fields, disciplines, even denominations or theological perspectives. Some of those voices seem not so very far away. The voices are the perspectives, experiences, and aspirations of the people churches are called to lead and serve. However, these voices may be farther away than they initially seem. A mountain on the horizon seems at first to be a short hike away. It is an illusion. Its size blinds us to its true distance. In the same way, the leaders of churches often assume that they understand the perspectives, experiences, and aspirations of the people they lead and serve only to discover a significant distance between their perception and the reality.

As I have noted, it is relatively easy to demonstrate that the leaders of churches lack clarity regarding the perceptions of the people they are called to lead and serve. When asked to estimate their members' priorities, church leaders are quite varied in their responses, with some thinking a particular issue is the highest priority for members and others thinking it is the lowest. What's more, they tend to hold their view uncritically, that is, with little awareness that the reality might be other than they imagine or that it is a reality they should seek to better understand. Like the mountain on the horizon, the reality is farther away from them than they realize. And this is exactly what one would expect. Leaders have contact with a relatively small number of those they lead and serve. It is natural that the proverbial blind man with a hand on the tusk of an elephant should generalize the tusk to the entire animal.

It is not simply what he does not know that is the problem; it is that he does not know what he does not know. The unlived life remains submerged as an unknown life and the commitment to discover it requires a journey.

The Journey of Jesus and Our Journey

For Christians, the journey of Jesus becomes the pattern for everyone seeking to discover the unlived life. Between his familiar life as carpenter and his unlived life as Messiah lies the wilderness with temptations designed to serve the dual purposes of derailing and clarifying his mission (Matt. 4:1–11; Luke 4:1–13). The power of this account is that it is not simply personal to Jesus. It is the pattern of our own struggle to emerge into a purposeful vitality. Unless a church possesses an awareness of these three temptations and a resolve to first be instructed by them and then overcome them, it is destined to push the rock of Sisyphus up the same ecclesiastical mountain only to find itself continually thrown back into the demoralizing diversions and debates that have become their unwanted companions.

The First Temptation: Institutional Hunger

The first temptation of Jesus, to turn stones into bread, finds its collective counterpart in the church's temptation to succumb to its *institutional hunger*. Institutional hunger expresses itself in a variety of cravings for the resources that will simply keep it alive. Like a human body that will actually deplete its bones of calcium to maintain the electrical circuitry that keeps its heart beating, institutional hunger begins sacrificing its mission simply to meet its own internally focused needs. If a church falls to this temptation, it will fail to emerge into its new life and will continually circle back to a deteriorated state of its previous one.

The strength of this temptation can hardly be overstated, but the signs of its operation are subtle. They can be recognized most clearly in how the institution deals with money. In most churches, morale is alarmingly low, with roughly half of its membership clearly positive about its work and a large percentage feeling like it is just going through the motions of religious activity. But as long as there are adequate financial reserves, no alarm is actually sounded. In fact, most churches will delay any action until they fall below some financial threshold, which finally serves as the trip wire for an explosion of concern. Unfortunately, for many churches, it is then too late. They have fallen below the critical mass required for any innovative ignition. For the rest, a severe repentance will be required to transform the worldly sorrow of lost prestige into an impetus for mission.

Like all the temptations, institutional hunger has the properties of quicksand. The deeper one sinks, the stronger the downward pull. Those churches where two-thirds of the membership indicate they are just going through the motions of religious activity often also insist that reaching new members is their highest priority! What kind of mission is it to bring people in need of God's grace and healing into an institution where they will be further demoralized and disillusioned? This is not only a-missional, it is also actually de-missional; it is a degraded mission in which new members are sought to feed the needs of the institution.

Leaders must be prepared to deal forcefully with this first temptation. Spotting it as it appears either in the evidence coming from the people they lead or in the structure of their own thinking is a necessary beginning. In the extreme case, better to lose building and chaplain in order to welcome new Christians into a universally purposeful and energized gathering around a kitchen table than enfold them into a demoralized remnant to which they also must finally succumb. Whatever positive spirit members may have when they join a church, the system will eventually reshape those attitudes to fit the contours of the membership as a whole. Better to give away the millions of an endowment to a body exuding the kingdom's protein into the world and amplify its signal than to use it all up in a slow drip over an extended ecclesiastical hospice.

Harsh though it may sound, to do otherwise is to fall into the orbit of a dark star that can only destroy us. Our Christian tradition leaves us well equipped to deal with sin through confession, repentance, and forgiveness. I recommend no less than trips to the altar; acknowledging wrongdoing in thought, word, and deed; pronouncing forgiveness; embracing one another in the peace of Christ; and setting about a different course in expressions of repentance. If, as Dietrich Bonhoeffer said, nothing can be more cruel than the tenderness that consigns another to his sin, how much more so to allow entire churches to continue in the downward path of the familiar when it destines them to forfeit the unlived life that is beckoning.[2]

The Second Temptation: The Tactical Shortcut

The second temptation is quite different but no less deadly. It is the temptation to a *tactical shortcut.* Jesus is invited to jump off the temple so that the angels can catch him a few inches above the pavement. The resulting spectacle holds the potential for winning over the crowds with nothing required beyond spectatorship. This is the siren's call: *All you need is the right charismatic leader.* The force of the temptation is not in the desire for a strong leader; it is the beguiling hope that with the right leader, the institution itself will not have to change.

After thirty years of researching hundreds of churches and religious institutions, I can say, nearly without exception, that churches where members indicate they are least willing to change are also the most miserable. Their misery makes them less willing to change and their reluctance to change makes them more miserable. What keeps them in this spiral? It is the hope that a temple-leaping leader of some description or another will come along and save them from the pain, and ultimately rob them of the unmatched blessing, of having to change. But this shortcut to vitality never works in the long run. If the church is unfortunate enough to find such a person, it is usually someone with personal issues that will exact a heavy price in the end. In my sojourn in Ireland, I saw a bumper sticker that said: "A shortcut is the longest distance between two points." A landscape covered with bogs and deeply creviced rocks just off the winding road burns this admonition into the consciousness at so many levels.

There is no shortcut to the vitality of a church where its people are clear about their purpose, are engaged in a life of service shaped around their God-breathed gifts and passions, are equipped to live in healthy relationships that are also self-correcting of contradictory behaviors, and live with an abiding sense of Presence that spills over into the lives of others who long for some sign of hope in a barren consumer landscape. The leadership team that delays this journey in hopes it can be avoided through a person or program has fallen under the spell of a temptation that will lift their church to a great height only to send it catapulting over a precipice.

Again, when leaders see that the people they serve are giving evidence of succumbing to this temptation or that it has taken root in the structure of their own thinking, they must be spiritually fortified to address it. In addition to confession and forgiveness, opportunities for repentance can be provided in spiritual formation offerings that address core spiritual competencies.

The Third Temptation: Transformational Naiveté

The third temptation is different still. It is the temptation to *transformational naiveté*. The devil shows Jesus all the kingdoms of the world and then offers them to him if he will but make a simple deal: "All this I will give you," he said, "if you will bow down and worship me" (Matt. 4:9). There is a dark side to the institution, but we are tempted to ignore it in the hope that it will simply go away. It will not. The dark side will destroy the essential unity of the body of Christ. It will wear leaders down, it will split people up, it will hem people in, it will burn people out. It will trample the souls of young sprouts seeking nourishment and light. It will turn the grounded wisdom of old souls into hard pavement.

The thought that this institutional dark side will simply yield to the growing vitality of the body and be joyful at its rebirth is naive. Affirmation alone is not sufficient to the task. I have encountered very few leaders of renewed churches and religious organizations who have not had to pass through a difficult season of confronting behaviors that the institution had come to tolerate. These behaviors fall into three broad categories: (1) inappropriate communication patterns, (2) contradictory expectations, and (3) unsustainable demands for attention. In the short run, the leadership must confront this side of the institution when no one else will, but this can only be done as a sprint, in order to prevent the burnout of the leader or the polarization of church by those for or against the "intolerant" pastor. In the long run, others must share the burden of this responsibility. The church must become a self-correcting system.

We are told that Jesus emerged from these three temptations in the power of the Spirit and began the ministry that emerged from his unlived life. The three temptations had not only failed to derail him but also actually made it safe for him to be successful. The power of Jesus' sojourn in the wilderness is not that it was simply personal to him. It is mythic. It gives every person insight into the psychic journey and gives *every* church insight into what they will face in moving toward the life they have not yet known.

In an evidence-based discernment process, leaders will discover evidence of these three temptations not only coming from the people they lead but also in the structure of their own thinking. Leaders best serve their people when they can normalize the experience of these temptations by explaining that these are common temptations faced by every church on the journey. The pull of their gravity is not a sign that we are on the wrong path. On the contrary, on the journey to the unlived life, the absence of these temptations should cause us to wonder if we have taken a wrong turn. We should also normalize the experience of failure coupled with the normal expressions of confession, forgiveness, repentance, and embracing one another in peace. Regression is normal. I am thinking of a church where the leaders have discovered through their organizational intelligence a deeply ingrained tendency to view the entire church through the filter of the pastor. Over the years, this has led them to call a series of deeply wounded leaders. Now they are in the process of a new search. Even with all they now know, they still catch themselves falling to the second temptation described above, the tactical shortcut. The difference is that they are aware of when they slip off the path and they take steps to get back on it . . . together. Only when churches have tamed their institutional hunger and transformed it into a missional impulse, only when they have embraced the change of heart, mind, and action that a new life will require, and only when they are prepared to confront the dark side of individual and corporate life can they be trusted with the transformational responsibility that God is calling them to today.

Creating Space for Fresh Insight

To successfully navigate these three temptations, it is imperative that leaders not only have access to organizational intelligence but also be open to seeing the landscape about them. It is difficult not to fall into a hole when the road you are traveling is pitch black. This leads to the second area requiring spiritual preparation: creating space in the mind and heart for fresh insight. Spiritually, a mind, like a parachute, can only work when it is open. We are guided in this task by the text in Genesis 3. Again, this powerful account is mythic. It is not simply the story of what happened to Adam and Eve; it is a map of the psychic landscape for everyone and for every church committed to taking a look in the mirror.

An essential Christian understanding of people is that they are created in the image of God. This image is expressed both through the individual and through the relationships, male and female, that compose a community. While not decisive, community is powerful in shaping individual behavior to either sustain the image of God or distort it. In support of this point, research has shown that individual attitudes are not a good predictor of actual behavior.[3] A person who does not have racist attitudes, for example, may behave as a racist if he or she is in a group that has those values. In the same way, Adam does not hold his own when his community (Eve) begins to deteriorate. Both Adam and Eve are commanded not to eat of the tree of the knowledge of good and evil. In response to the seduction of the serpent, Eve disobeys and eats the fruit. She then models that behavior to Adam. Eve represents the only human community Adam has available to him. Consequently, he disobeys as well. Eve's failure does not provide Adam with an excuse for his behavior, but it does offer insight about the role that community plays in shaping his life.

Sin distorts the individual's self-perception and the community's self-perception as well. This distorted self-perception is represented in the creation account by various defensive behaviors symbolized by hiding behind fig leaves (Gen. 3:7). The New Testament expresses this issue using the metaphor of physical blindness. The Christian community, the body of Christ, is subject to the same perceptual errors even though it is guided by the Holy Spirit.

Some parts of the life of a particular church are easily acknowledged and *shared*.[4] This is the information we are most likely to surface in conversation. It usually has a low level of complexity. Intricate patterns are difficult to discern by the human mind in such settings.

Other parts of the community's life are *hidden* from one another and the larger community. Members entering the leadership of a church for the first time often express surprise at the less savory aspects of church life they discover just below the surface. On the positive side, there is almost always a significant amount of potential that lies hidden. In nearly every church, roughly 30 percent of members indicate they have something to give but don't know how to give it.

Still other aspects of the church are *unknown* even to its leaders. It is impossible for a single individual to know the collective perspective of the entire church through informal conversations. In many cases, leaders don't know what they don't know. Redemption and renewal requires a reversal of these perceptual distortions. In order for individuals and communities to grow, they must recover a more accurate understanding of where they really are. It is impossible to give people directions to a particular location if they cannot tell you where they are! Scripture often places before us a lofty vision of the church with all its possibilities, for example, as the bride of Christ without spot or wrinkle. However, without a clear understanding of the starting point, a vision devolves into a fantasy. Therefore, it is important to recognize that Scripture also calls us to a realistic self-assessment: "For by the grace given me I say to every one of you: Do not think of yourself more highly than you ought, but rather think of yourself with sober judgment, in accordance with the measure of faith God has given you" (Romans 12:3).

In their responses to the presence of God, Adam and Eve symbolize a set of predictable human tendencies for leaders entering into an evidence-based discernment process: shame, denial, and blame.

Our first tendency is to respond with *shame.* Discovering that the people in the church you lead are not as hospitable to one another as you thought can feel like a failure. If we allow this to become a wound to the ego (Edging God Out), we are more likely to despair, dismiss the information, or hide from what it might require of us.

This leads to the second tendency: *denial.* I know of a hospital that conducted an extensive survey of patients to evaluate different aspects of patient care. When the results came back, the doctors had a "first" rating. The physicians saw the rating and went into a state of rejoicing. "We're number one!" they chanted. What they failed to realize was that "first" meant they were in the first percentile. In other words 99 percent of the hospitals in their peer group had *higher* scores on the quality of their care. They were rated dead last. Suddenly, the cheers turned to dismissals of the validity of the results.

The final tendency is to *blame.* "The woman whom you gave to me . . ." says Adam (Gen. 3:12). Blaming can take many forms and can land on a wide variety of targets, ranging from a pastor to fellow leaders to external circumstances to the assessment process itself. Each of these temptations threatens to impede the flow of insight, thwart the creative spirit, and block our birthright as purposeful, vital churches.

All truth is God's truth. That God is loving and gracious, that $e = mc^2$, and that curious tendency of all children to giggle at peekaboo, all these are expressions of God's truth. The process of discovering God's truth, in any of its many forms, always has an element of revelation to it as if one were being shown something. Using the vernacular of our day, our own personal discoveries have the quality of "a light coming on." This is also the language used by Jesus as he describes the discovery of God's nature and purposes in the world. "Whoever follows me will never walk in darkness, but will have the light of life" (John 8:12).

Organizational Intelligence as Revelation

Discovering the perspectives, experiences, and aspirations of a church is also one of revelation and has the quality of moving from darkness into light. "A light comes on" as people come to understand aspects of the entire body of Christ that they could not possibly have known from the relatively small number of interactions that characterize the day-to-day relationships in most organizations. This process of reality moving out of the shadows and into the light is a spiritual journey.

As a spiritual journey, it has all the elements one would expect. There are insights that evoke a liberating "aha" as connections are uncovered that were not intuitively obvious. Some aspects of the process tell us nothing new, but they express what we do know using language that enables us to get a firmer grasp. Sometimes the need for healing is revealed in the often painful and occasionally urgent relational wounds that come to light. There are the common resistances that we all experience, the sense of inferiority or shame or fear that tempts us to retreat into the perceived safety of the darkness. Finally, there is the concrete action that must root itself in the earth of any spiritual journey and express itself in fruit for the kingdom of God.

The fulfillment of a spiritual journey ultimately hinges not on the research design but upon the spiritual practice that surrounds it. Without this spiritual practice, insights degenerate into trivia, wounds are probed but not healed, resistances harden into defensiveness and denial, and the promised new life fails to materialize as an incarnate reality. King David's greatest loss of life was not to an enemy but to his own inability to manage information and keep it disentangled from his own ego. In 2 Samuel 21, he decides to take a census, presumably to use the information as a way of feeding his own pride. As a result, seventy thousand men died along with the unreported deaths of women and children.

Evidence-Based Discernment and Spiritual Practice

For these reasons, it is critical that an evidence-based approach be interwoven with a robust spiritual practice including prayer, reflection, confession, study, and worship. Because an evidence-based assessment generates a symbolic narrative, the leadership team must ponder several questions:

- How do we deal with our stories? (While individuals' contributions to the assessment are confidential, the congregation's corporate story will be quite public.)
- How might the disclosure of our corporate story bring insight, healing, and renewal?
- In the past, how have we dealt with surprises, with things we thought were true but we discovered were not?
- In that same past, how have we dealt with our wounds, our resistances, and our tendency to intellectualize as an escape from change?
- How do we find access to the grace of God in this process of discovery so that our journey might be one expressive of Jesus, full of grace *and* truth?

Building on a foundation of God's grace and having considered what lies ahead, we are now prepared to open ourselves to organizational intelligence. The apostle Paul uses the word *aim* six times to describe the Christian life from the perspective of hitting a target. The next chapter engages one of the critical questions of evidence-based discernment: What is the target we are attempting to hit?

Discussion Questions

1. In this chapter I assert that many churches have an unlived life that members sense but are not yet living because they are afraid of the changes it may require. Do you believe that your church has an unlived life? How would you describe it?

2. This chapter identifies three temptations that can trip leaders up in discovering the life that God has for the church. Which of these do you believe is the greatest temptation for your church?

3. The primary obstacles to organizational intelligence are not intellectual or technology-related but emotional and spiritual (shame, denial, blame). What spiritual practices and resources might help a church overcome these obstacles?

PART 2

The Structure of Organizational Intelligence

CHAPTER 5

The Strike Zone: What Your Church Is Aiming For

*I would not give a fig for the simplicity on this side
of complexity, but I would give my life for the simplicity
on the other side of complexity.*

—Oliver Wendell Holmes Sr., American author, 1809–1894

What makes a good baseball pitch? A professional ball player could elucidate the many different aspects of a good pitch, ranging from the speed of the throw to the deception of the batter. But it is all for naught if the pitcher cannot throw a ball through the strike zone. In addition, players must have a common understanding of how it will be determined that the target has been hit: that's called an umpire.

Umpires are not the most popular figures in baseball. There is the story of God and the devil choosing up sides for a game of baseball. When God boasts that heaven is sure to win because they have Joe DiMaggio, Mickey Mantle, and all the greatest players, the devil responds, "Yes, but I have all the umpires."

Helping people get clear about whether they are hitting or missing an important target is not always popular. But it is essential. If you do not know what the target is, you hit it every time and miss it every time, depending upon how the target has been defined. Every fruitful team effort requires a clear target and a way of determining if the target has been hit.

My Biases

So what is the strike zone for a church? *Everything in evidence-based discernment hinges upon how we answer that question.* Before I offer my candidates for that answer, let me state my biases.

First, I am biased in favor of the *witness of members* regarding their experience in the church as a measure of health and vitality, and I am biased against count data alone. One reason for this is that changes in count data (like worship attendance) are generally downstream from changes in the experiences of members. Positive, faith-filled members are likely to have a correspondingly positive impact upon worship attendance, for example. The converse is often not the case. Members of churches that are simply growing numerically do not always appreciate what that growth has required or how it is affecting their personal experience of the church. Some (though certainly not all) churches that are growing numerically are accumulating a backlog of discontent that will eventually poison the spirit of the church and arrest further growth. By the time count data reflects this, the damage has been done.

Second, I am biased in favor of a *concrete, measurable approach* to health and vitality and biased against vague, conceptual definitions that, while not making anyone uncomfortable, are also useless in determining whether a church is moving forward or backward. In an attempt to avoid bruised egos, we in the church have for years skirted the difficult conversations about the sad state of many congregations. Unfortunately, we have simply delayed the discomfort and deferred the responsibility for communicating the message of the sad state of our congregations to the external environment. It is tragic that the conversations about a church's vitality often do not begin until the merciless hand of a changing environment begins to pull it under. The long-term practice of avoiding concrete, measurable ways of assessing health contributes to a church's silent demise.

Third, I am biased in favor of an onsite *joie de vivre*. The phrase is difficult to fully capture in English. It is not merely the trifle of happiness. It is a comprehensive joy, a philosophy of life that involves one's whole being. It embraces the joy of conversations, the joy of eating, the joy of purpose, the joy of the moment; it may be seen as the joy of everything. If we have evidence that a church is vital and healthy, I want to be able to get onto a plane, fly to that city or town, wade into its people, and *sense* that there is something in the air that is better felt than described.

Finally, I am biased in favor of *simplicity*. It is said that the Old Testament contains 613 commands, all aimed at leading a holy life.

God said, "That is not simple enough."

So Moses condensed it to ten.

God said, "That is not simple enough."

Jesus boiled it down to two. Love God. Love your neighbor. Jesus distinguished between the target (the ultimate goal: love God) and the trajectory (how you get there: love your neighbor). The 613 laws continue to be important but only as paths that lead to loving God, loving others. The paths may change, but the target never does.

What Is a Healthy Church?

A healthy, vital church, like a healthy, vital individual, expresses itself in the world in many and varied ways, which cannot be fully anticipated and therefore cannot be reliably benchmarked. This is why a discussion about the behaviors of a healthy church almost always devolves into a laundry list that has something on it for everyone but has little utility. If we reviewed all the literature, we would probably discover 613 criteria to measure the vitality of a church but that no one would ever use. It is simply too complicated. How do we distinguish between the target and the path?

I would like to propose that the targets are *satisfaction* and *energy*. The evidence suggests that a church is vital and healthy when members bear witness to their experience in the body of Christ as one that is both satisfying and energizing. Notice that this definition meets my first criteria: it is based on the *witness of members*, you can't *count* it. Yet, it still meets my second criteria: it is *concrete* and *measurable*. It meets my third criteria of an onsite *joie de vivre*. I have boarded airplanes and traveled around the country for the joy of experiencing these churches. Finally, it meets my fourth criteria. It is *simple*.

I have found that I can get a read on the health and vitality of a church by asking two simple questions:

- How satisfied are you with what is happening in your church overall?
- What do you perceive is the level of energy and excitement in your church?

If you are a member of a leadership team and your team knows the answers to just those two questions for the members of your church, you have acquired an enormous amount of organizational intelligence that provides insight into (1) where your church is, (2) what strategies are likely to be effective, (3) what leadership tasks need to be accomplished, and (4) what kind of leader might be a good fit. If you have clarity about the answers to just those two questions, you know more about the general state of your church than 95 percent of the church leaders across the country.

Satisfaction and energy are two different but related factors. We will begin with *satisfaction*. For many people, the word *satisfied* has an unseemly quality to it because they associate it with self-satisfaction and it smacks of conceit. The word actually has its roots in the Latin *satisfacere*, which means "content," and *satis,* which means "enough." In actual experience, we find that in churches where members indicate a high level of satisfaction the community usually reflects the Hebrew *shalom*, an expansive term that includes completeness, wholeness, health, peace, welfare, safety, soundness, tranquility, prosperity, perfectness, fullness, rest, harmony, and the absence of agitation or discord. Contrary to common belief, the research indicates that high satisfaction is never achieved by simply pandering to the self-interests of members. It is more accurately a shalom created by a number of components that combine to produce a sense of wholeness.

In contrast, the word *energy* does not cast the shadow that *satisfied* does. In its Latin and Greek roots, it does not have quite the material, physical connotation that *energy* has today, but is nuanced in the direction of "work" or "force of engagement." This is the way I'm using the word when I talk about congregational health and vitality. A high-energy church is one where members experience a compelling purpose or message combined with a high level of engagement, in contrast to a church where members are simply watching others or going through the motions of religious activity.

Energy is distinct from satisfaction. You may have a car that evokes satisfaction (you love its shape, color, interior) . . . and is totally out of gas (energy). Sometimes folks are in a church that they sincerely love (they love the people, the liturgy, the history, the mission, and so forth), but they are out of energy. Conversely, people can be very energized about their engagement in a particular aspect of a church and yet quite dissatisfied with how things are being run overall. Satisfaction tends to be an operational quality. Energy tends to be more about purpose, meaning, and the capacity for action.

Four Distinct Vitality States

Our consulting firm has found that members bear witness to four different vitality states: (1) low satisfaction and high energy; (2) low satisfaction and low energy, (3) high satisfaction and low energy, and (4) high satisfaction and high energy. These are represented in figure 5.1. I call this diagram the *Energy-Satisfaction Map*®. The *Energy-Satisfaction Map*® plots the location of a particular church on a grid where the level of overall satisfaction (shalom) is indicated on the horizontal axis and the level of overall energy (force of engagement) is indicated on the vertical axis. It is important to emphasize that this is a witness-driven map. It reflects what members are saying about their experience in the church overall. Again, you know where your church is on this map if you know how your members would answer these two questions:

- How satisfied are you with what is happening in your church overall?
- What do you perceive is the level of energy and excitement in your church?

Each of these quadrants represents a specific church state and a distinct experience for members.

Low Satisfaction High Energy	High Satisfaction High Energy
Low Satisfaction Low Energy	High Satisfaction Low Energy

Figure 5.1. The Energy-Satisfaction Map

Chaotic Systems

We characterize low-satisfaction, high-energy churches as *chaotic systems*. They generally have an abundance of "force of engagement" but lack shalom. These tend to be churches with a number of distinct, rather autonomous centers of activity. The activities may center on a particular person, staff or lay, an internal ministry such as music or education, or an external ministry related to justice or evangelism. They are characterized by a high degree of subgroup loyalty, a significant level of commitment, and a distinct or creative approach to their work. However, their allegiance to a larger vision, governance system, or overall leader is often low. The result is a church where members experience a high level of energy that is out of alignment with a central purpose. It is a bit like a gasoline engine where fuel is exploding outside the cylinders; instead of driving the entire car forward, it is creating brilliant, random, noisy flashes here, there, and everywhere. Efforts to restore alignment are met with resistance. Conflict ensues, which lowers satisfaction.

Recovery Systems

We characterize low-satisfaction, low-energy churches as *recovery systems*. These tend to be churches where any combination of factors has led to an erosion of morale. Often the stated goal of these churches is reaching new members. However, it is difficult to make a compelling case to prospective members in an organization where two-thirds of existing members indicate they are simply going through the motions of religious activity and less than half are clearly positive about the way the church is being operated.

I was fortunate to sit under the instruction Dr. Roberta Hestenes at Fuller Seminary. One of her quips that I found particularly memorable addresses this issue at a personal level: "Before you decide to tell someone about Jesus, make sure you are fun to be with!" Churches do well when they take this counsel to heart at a corporate level. Jesus had little truck with religion that simply made people more burdened and alienated.

Low Satisfaction High Energy **CHAOTIC**	High Satisfaction High Energy **TRANSFORMATIONAL**
RECOVERY Low Satisfaction Low Energy	**STATIC** High Satisfaction Low Energy

Figure 5.2. Four Church Systems

While some people in recovery systems realize that change is imperative, most find it difficult to change familiar patterns of behavior. Unfortunately, those patterns are often self-defeating. As in chaotic systems, in recovery systems conflict becomes difficult to manage, which further erodes morale. When internal resources are finally depleted, leaders of recovery system churches often turn to the larger church for funding to keep the doors open, but this is usually only a temporary fix.

Static Systems

I characterize high-satisfaction, low-energy churches as *static systems*. Static systems are similar to recovery systems in that they are generally stuck in patterns that are not fruitful. In contrast to recovery systems, they have made their peace with where they are, which sometimes gives them relatively low levels of conflict (and high shalom). Members in a static system can be quite congenial and welcoming, but this does little to reduce the steady hemorrhage of resources. Members know the church may be spiraling in an unstoppable descent, but they just don't have the energy to do much about it.

Transformational Systems

Finally, I characterize high-satisfaction, high-energy churches as *transformational systems.* In contrast with most mainline churches, transformational systems have discovered ways to be vibrant and healthy in spite of national or regional trends for churches in mainline denominations (for example, the Episcopal Church, the Evangelical Lutheran Church in America, the Presbyterian Church [USA], the United Church of Christ). It is impossible to predict the precise ways that this vitality will express itself through a particular congregation. The more tangible expressions include an external focus, a distinctive mission, and an influx of people who bear witness to transformation. The more intangible expressions might be described as a corporate spiritual zest; encounter-driven, inspired worship; healthy, healing, meaningful relationships; purposeful activity in the world; a sense of being at the right place at the right time, both individually and corporately; and a nearly palpable atmosphere of well-being about the grounds.

Transformational churches come in all sizes, contexts, and theological perspectives. I am thinking now about a transformational church that is quite progressive and thriving in an urban environment in Pittsburgh, Pennsylvania. Another comes to mind that is a smaller, moderately conservative church in a small town in southern Louisiana. Still another is a very large, evangelical church in central Michigan. Similar to an individual, as the vitality and health of a church are diminished, so are its options for expression. Healthy, vital churches produce fruit that varies from community to community. Demoralized churches tend to look the same.

This is not meant to imply that transformational churches do not have their own growth edges. Some transformational churches need to work on the spiritual vitality of their individual members. Others have a rate of giving that is dismal compared to their resources. Some could improve their level of hospitality and welcome. Here's the point: it is much easier to work on all these things from a position where members feel good about themselves and energized about what they are doing.

Different Strategies, Leadership Tasks, and Leader Types

What is important to the message of this book is that *each of these systems requires a different strategic plan, a different set of leadership tasks, and in some cases, a different kind of leader.* Figure 5.3 illustrates that while the goal of churches in each system may be the same (becoming more vital), they start from different places and, therefore, must follow a different trajectory.

Chaotic systems need long-term strategies that will create alignment of the independent activity centers with a central mission. This will require some shifting of loyalty from individual, and often autonomous, activity centers to the larger church and its leadership. The tasks that are required to do this include identifying common values, developing a shared vision, learning to work cross-functionally, accepting a level of accountability and discipline, and managing the allocation of resources. The leadership needs to be able to weather short-term reactions to a loss of control and usually some losses of members. I call this leadership style *the union negotiator.* It is not work for the faint of heart.

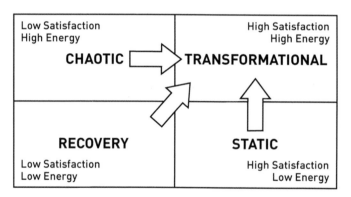

Figure 5.3. Trajectories toward Vitality

Recovery systems need to be exposed to a collection of fresh strategic and tactical resources that can help jump-start a turnaround. Increasingly, these will not be books off a shelf or packaged programs. They will be ministry approaches that others are finding fruitful in real time. Such real-time resourcing will require a virtual network of church leaders who have overcome their historic propensity toward isolation, who are developing organizational intelligence at the regional level and can share best practices as they are discovered. By the time these get packaged and published in books, many are already out of date (alas!).

The tasks that are required to turn the congregation around include a clarification of purpose, spiritual formation, equipping leaders, a shift to an external focus, and tactical flexibility. In many cases, recovery churches need to focus on the basics of Christian discipleship shaped by a contemporary context. I call this leadership style *the line coach,* because a line coach in football is focused on doing a few basic things extremely well. The leadership needs to be able to embrace this journey with faith, an optimism toward the future, a spiritual zest, and a thirst for learning.

Static systems, on the other hand, often don't have the motivation to engage any of these tasks, because they are more or less satisfied with where they are. If the level of energy is only moderately low, efforts at renewing a sense of purpose can be effective. Churches deeper in the static quadrant require a more radical approach. They often need some bypass strategy that will build a new congregation from scratch around the existing one. The tasks that are required to do this include new church development, straddled and segmented pastoral leadership,[1] space and resource negotiation for multiple congregations that share the same space, and, eventually, reintegration. I call the leadership style needed for this system *the triage nurse,* because the leaders have to be able to make difficult decisions about what to focus on, what to let go, what to help live, and what to let die. This requires entrepreneurial leadership combined with chaplaincy, a combination unlikely to be found in a single person.

Finally, transformational systems have very different strategic and leadership needs. Their positive morale and organizational capacities place a stewardship responsibility upon their shoulders: "From everyone who has been given much, much will be demanded; and from the one who has been entrusted with much, much more will be asked" (Luke 12:48). As member satisfaction reaches 70 percent and energy reaches 85 percent, these churches cross a transformational threshold where strategic initiatives for mentoring, church planting, cataloguing of best practices, and succession planning must be considered. I call this leadership style *the field marshal,* because it requires optimizing a large array of strategic resources. While recovery churches are often seeking expertise, the expertise in transformational churches is often unconscious and leaders will need to bring their competence to consciousness before it can be shared. This also can be challenging work.

There we have it: four different systems, four different vitality states, four different strategic concerns, four different sets of leadership tasks. Which one should be considered is a matter of having an accurate compass reading on the starting point. Now we begin to see why evidence-based discernment is so critical. For while we might assume that leaders have a clear idea of how members are experiencing the church, we have seen they do not. In fact, it is likely that in any group of leaders you could take any quadrant and find folks who would make a case that the church is in that quadrant.

This is the point that should not be missed: a large amount of organizational intelligence can be derived from a modest effort if the right information is collected in a reliable manner. Does your leadership team know the answers to those two questions?

The Strike Zone Defined

Now we are clear about the strike zone. It is a church where 70 percent of the members bear witness to being clearly satisfied with the church and 85 percent of the members bear witness to a level of excitement and energy in the church. (See figure 5.4.)

How would the church of Jesus Christ be different today if this were the target that every pastor, staff member, lay leader, and member aspired to hit? Before we scramble about trying to find a reason why this is impossible for *our* church, let me just remind you that such churches already exist and they are

- of every size;
- of every theological persuasion;
- in small town, urban, and suburban environments; and
- financially well off and of humble means.

You may be wrestling with the fact that in this entire discussion of health and vitality I have not mentioned some activities that are core to the Christian faith, things like worship, discipleship, Christian education and formation, mission, social justice, evangelism, hospitality, peacemaking, preaching, and facilities. Where do these come in?

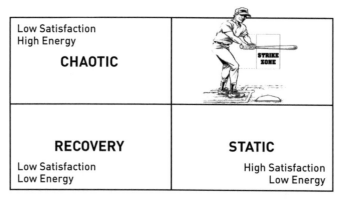

Figure 5.4. Defining the Strike Zone: Aiming for a Transformational System

A Gas Gauge Is Not a Gas Tank

The fact that we are measuring vitality through satisfaction and energy does not mean that a church can acquire these by merely seeking satisfaction and energy. A gas gauge is not a gas tank. It can tell us when we are running on empty but not where the nearest gas station is located. As I have listened to the witness of thousands of members from hundreds of churches, I have gained some insight into the activities that lead to higher energy and satisfaction. They are byproducts of other activities, and vital, healthy churches are generally aware of this. Some of these were discussed chapter 3 and will be further explored in chapter 6. They include the following:

Vital worship
Lifelong learning
Spiritual formation that fits complex lifestyles
An open leadership system
Quality relationships
Flexibility

You might wonder, isn't it possible that some churches that are simply self-focused will score high on satisfaction and energy? It is possible that some might, but to assume this is generally true does a disservice to those churches that have actually found a pathway to authentic vitality. It also encourages a culture that actually penalizes and marginalizes effective churches. This, I believe is the greater risk. In the parable of the wheat and the tares, Jesus warns us that any evaluative methodology that renders us chronically obsessed with "bad seed" will inevitably destroy the "good seed" as well. The suspicion that every high-satisfaction, high-energy church is simply self-focused is not only refuted by the research but it also plays into the shadows of human envy and competition. Even in the worst case, a church that is enthusiastically self-focused always has the possibility of a repentance that will redirect its focus and rechannel its resources. But a church that has shed most of its members and resources over years because it is chronically demoralized and unhappy sooner or later falls below the threshold of recovery.

If I am the leader of a church with a more progressive theological orientation, I want the church to be as high in shalom and force of engagement as possible in order to optimize the church's impact in the community on the social issues and justice activities we deem important. If I am the leader of a church with a more evangelical theological orientation, I want the church to be as high in shalom and force of engagement as possible in order to bring people to a personal relationship with Christ and develop them as individual disciples.

This target works well not only for the church but also for leadership groups within the church. If the leadership function is not healthy, sooner or later it is likely to manifest itself in the congregation. The goal is to develop high energy and satisfaction in these three areas:

- The congregation
- The leadership team (usually defined as the board and clergy)
- The staff (in larger churches)

Again, high satisfaction is different from self-satisfaction. When we look at high-energy, high-satisfaction churches and teams, we see the opposite of the consumer-driven, narcissistic creatures that many imagine. The members in low-energy, low-satisfaction churches tend to be more focused on internal issues like reaching new members, raising more money, and improving worship. Members in high-energy, high-satisfaction churches tend to be more externally focused. The particular form this external focus takes varies depending upon the church and the context. In some churches, it might be international mission. In another, it might be services to people who are marginalized. Still other high-energy, high-satisfaction churches focus on advocacy for social change.

With the answers to two simple questions, we have defined both the strike zone—a transformational system—and how far off that strike zone we are hitting, that is, the other quadrant (static, recovery, chaos,) in which a church may find itself. That is helpful information, but it does not give us any insight into what we need to do in order to pitch better.

That's in the next chapter.

Discussion Questions

1. I assert that the fundamewntal health of a church, regardless of size, setting, or context, can be reliably ascertained from two pieces of information, the level of satisfaction (shalom) and the level of energy. What do you like about this definition of health? Have you ever experienced a church firsthand that exhibited high satisfaction and energy that you would judge fundamentally unsound or sick?

2. The chapter describes four church states or systems: transformational, static, recovery, and chaos. Overall, which state best describes your church? How could you know for sure? What is positive about being in that state? What is challenging about being in that state?

3. I assert that there is a difference between being satisfied and being self-satisfied. Do you think there is a difference? Do you think it is possible for a church to develop a high level of satisfaction simply by trying harder and harder to be satisfied?

CHAPTER 6

From Least-Energy to Most-Likely-to-Succeed Solutions

*You can never solve a problem with the same kind of thinking
that created the problem in the first place.*
—Albert Einstein, German physicist and philosopher, 1879–1955

Bruce Larson in his book *Wind and Fire* tells about a National Football League championship game many years ago in which Dallas was playing Green Bay. The game was dubbed "The Ice Bowl." Green Bay was behind five points, with just seconds to play. Green Bay had the ball on the Dallas one foot line and it was fourth down. Everything hinged on that last play. In the huddle, the quarterback of the Packers, Bart Starr, turned to Jerry Kramer, the offensive guard, and said, "Jerry, if you can move Jethro Pugh twelve inches to the left, you will make fifteen thousand dollars." Jerry Kramer was clear about what he needed to do: move Jethro Pugh twelve inches to the left. Jerry responded. Jethro was moved. Green Bay won.

Leaders not only need to be clear about the target they need to hit, they also must have a clear understanding of the factors that must be addressed in order to achieve the goal. It is not enough to know that the goal of a football game is to score points. It is critical to know what needs to be moved and by how much.

Avoiding Least-Energy Solutions

If you talk with the average leader of a church in the United States, you will likely hear that it is difficult to get enough people to serve in the ministries of the church. The actual evidence reveals that one in four members of a typical church feels like he or she has something to give the church but doesn't know how to give it. This means that roughly fifteen million people feel underutilized by the churches they attend. This is another example of where the perception of leaders diverges sharply from the actual evidence. Leaders perceive that members are tapped out, while millions are looking for a way to make a contribution consistent with their motivations and abilities. Why is this? It is partly because leaders do not have available to them the organizational intelligence that will enable them to invest their energy in the right places.

Churches, like all organizations, tend to define a problem by the least-energy solution. Let us continue the discussion with the issue of recruitment. When churches find that they need more people to serve in key positions, they rarely engage in a thorough process of identifying the factors in the shortage, ranking those factors in importance, and developing an action plan to address the top one or two. As a result, they often develop a recruitment solution that relies heavily upon general publicity. The solution implies that the problem is a lack of awareness and assumes that a large percentage of people read church publications. A deeper analysis of the problem would probably reveal that the factors in the shortage are these:

1. Many people do not invest their scarce discretionary time to read church publications.
2. Appeals for support in newsletters or other articles are generally the least effective method of recruitment. (Research has shown this to be the case.)
3. The general recruitment approach in many congregations is inefficient and redundant, with many people engaged in recruiting the same pool of people to different areas.
4. Members look for avenues of involvement that are congruent with their gifts and motivations.
5. The church is *slot focused* rather than *ministry focused*; that is, the congregation tends to help people find their ministry in order to fill existing roles in the church. But for many people in the church, what they have to give will not fit into a standard slot, an existing role.
6. People have had bad experiences serving in churches and need reassurance that it won't develop into a pattern.

Approaches that take these factors into account are much more likely to be fruitful in the long term. Even though they may be more work in the short term, most leaders will choose these alternative approaches to recruiting people to serve if they are led through a disciplined process that helps them stay focused. In the absence of a good process, leaders will often revert to a solution along the path of least resistance . . . that does not work.

Let's return to our target (strike zone). Simply stated, our goal is to create a high-satisfaction (shalom), high-energy (force of engagement) church, which we define as a church where at least 70 percent of the members indicate that they are satisfied with the church and at least 85 percent of its people bear witness to excitement and energy among the faith community. Again, whether you have a more progressive or liberal vision for the impact of the church you lead or a more conservative or evangelical vision, you will need your church functioning at this level to achieve impact. One promise of evidence-based discernment is that it helps leaders develop clarity about what is most important for them to address in order to create a healthy, vital church.

I have now stated several times that this level of vitality cannot be achieved simply by giving people what they want any more than a company can achieve high morale among its employees by simply giving them more and more money. So what are those factors that lead to greater vitality? Every leadership team needs to generate its own organizational intelligence so that it can develop its own clarity. However, when we look at the intelligence from hundreds of churches, we can identify six characteristics that all high-satisfaction, high-energy churches have in common.

1. They have developed a worship experience that members overwhelming affirm as high quality and outstanding.
2. They have developed an open leadership system that is not tightly controlled by a few people.
3. They have developed a membership with a thirst for lifelong learning and growth.
4. They have developed a ministry of spiritual formation that fits the complex lifestyles of their people.
5. Members overwhelmingly affirm quality relationships that create a positive, friendly atmosphere in the church.
6. Members bear witness to a high level of flexibility rather than simply sticking to established ways of doing things.

All six of these factors are important, but the weight of their contribution to the vitality of a church varies. Their weight is reflected in the bar chart found in figure 6.1 (the longer the bar, the more important the factor). This is called a fishbone analysis, since the pattern of the bars resembles the bones of a fish.

A fishbone analysis helps a leadership team know where it needs to focus scarce resources. If a leadership team can make changes in only one area, where should they focus? Worship. Even if it is easier to make changes in other areas, unless members feel they are having a meaningful and inspiring worship experience, it will be difficult for a church to develop a higher level of energy and vitality. Without that vitality, it will be difficult to make the case that new members should join.

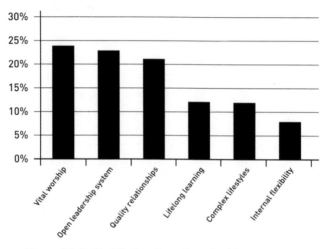

Figure 6.1. Critical Factors in an Energized Congregation

Churches of every size can develop a worship experience that is meaningful and inspiring not only to longtime members but also to those from the local community who are most likely to walk through the doors. But developing that worship experience takes more than the pastor.

Name of Church:	*Ormond Beach Presbyterian Church*
Vitality Status:	*Transformational*
Member focus:	*Ministry-focused*
Critical success factors:	*Inclusion of persons from different walks of life*
Level of criticality:	*Very low*
Priority Focus:	*Hearth and Home*

Figure 6.2. Ormond Beach Presbyterian Church Organizational Intelligence
Profile. For a definition of terms, please see the glossary in appendix A.

Ormond Beach Presbyterian Church, near Daytona Beach, Florida, has an energy level that is higher than 98 percent of the churches in the United States. (See figure 6.2.) How have they accomplished that? One major factor is the power of the worship experience. With a Sunday worship attendance of about 190 people and a large snowbird population, the church doesn't have the vast resources of a megachurch to invest into a jazzed up, high-tech worship service. Yet the members of this church rank their worship experience higher than 98 percent of the churches in the country, including many large, wealthy congregations. When I asked how they had learned to create such a vibrant worship experience, they had several answers. One was the fact that they annually send about *twenty* people to the worship conference at Montreat, North Carolina. That's a commitment to a most-likely-to-succeed solution. Above all else, the evidence is compelling that a leadership team must commit itself to creating a vital worship experience for those who enter. (As we shall see in a later chapter, a younger cohort wants worship linked to community impact.)

Fingerprints

Every person has fingerprints that look roughly the same. Yet the fingerprints of a particular person are unique.

One value of organizational intelligence is that it not only gives us insight into the general patterns of all churches across the country but it also identifies the patterns that are unique to a particular congregation. With that intelligence in hand, leaders can engage in a discernment process using most-likely-to-succeed strategies. Or they can revert to impression-driven processes and least-energy solutions. It is so easy for any of us to look in the mirror, walk away, and forget what we look like.

One evening a policeman came upon a little boy on his hands and knees. When the policeman asked what he was doing, the little boy replied, "I am looking for a quarter I lost."

"Where did you lose it?" he asked.

"On Third Street," the boy answered.

"Son, this is Fifth Street," the policeman replied.

"I know," said the boy. "But there is more light here."

It is tempting to abandon an evidence-based process when looking for solutions in other places is easier.

Early in my consultant career, I was working with a library that wanted to gain clarity about its mission. After about a day with the leadership, the consultant team discovered that they had been trying to get clarity for about twenty years. It dawned on us that they could never find clarity, because searching where it might actually be found was too difficult for them. Finally we came back to them with the question, "What do you think is standing in the way of getting clarity?"

"Fear of conflict" was the answer.

What they were looking for—clarity about their mission—was on Third Street. They kept looking on Fifth Street because it was easier—there they could avoid conflict—but they could never find the focus they needed. It kept them from having to engage in the difficult conversations and from clarity about purpose.

The promise of evidence-based discernment is that it helps us know where and what to engage. The challenge of evidence-based discernment is that it calls us to engage in what author Susan Scott calls *Fierce Conversations*. If a leadership team consistently avoids the difficult conversations, it must not be surprised when the chronic decline of the church drops below a sustainable threshold.

The Trap of Pastoral Care

It is surprising for many church folks to learn that there is little evidence indicating that the quality of pastoral care provided by the pastor is a major factor in creating vital churches. In over twenty years of collecting organizational intelligence from thousands of members and hundreds of congregations, I have almost never seen a church where the care provided by the pastor to individuals was the leading driver of either satisfaction or energy for the church overall. Clearly, our experience would suggest that pastoral care is important. So why doesn't it show up as a clear factor in vital churches?

I would suggest that pastoral care is like food. Food is essential to life and health. However, once a person has an adequate supply of nutritional food, more food does not make that person more healthy. Past a certain point, more food actually makes a person *less* healthy. At an even higher level of consumption, food is a killer. More makes less. Put another way, an absence of food is a *dissatisfier*, but once a person has had a sufficient amount, more food doesn't make a person more satisfied. Once a pastor provides an adequate level of pastoral care, more pastoral care does not make the church stronger, it actually cripples it by creating dependencies. In addition, an overinvestment in dissatisfiers distracts leaders from the more powerful *satisfiers*, that is, factors where more is almost always better.

One major task of a leader is to distinguish between dissatisfiers and true satisfiers. For example, when it comes to the morale of a staff, the evidence is clear: money is a dissatisfier but not a satisfier. Once a staff member is paid a fair salary, more money will not increase the staff member's morale.

Absent of true satisfiers, more money will simply create a situation in which the person may say, "I hate this job, but I can't afford to leave it." It is called the "golden handcuffs." In those cases, more money actually makes the person feel trapped, decreases self-esteem, and lowers morale. Like food, more makes less.

In contrast, making significant achievements is a true satisfier. The more a staff team believes it is achieving something significant, the more energized it becomes. More makes more.

The evidence suggests the aspects of a pastor's work that have the biggest impact on church vitality are these:

Bringing out the best in people

Articulating a clear vision

Communicating in a way that keeps people informed and connected

A little reflection suggests why this might be so. Take the first factor, bringing out the best in people. It is difficult to imagine a situation where bringing too much good out of too many people would be a bad. More makes more. It is also difficult to imagine a situation where a clearer vision might be a worse vision. The more clearly the pastor articulates the vision and helps every member and group of members understand how they contribute to that vision, the more energized the congregation. More makes more. Overcommunicating is almost always a plus, especially in an age of competing messages. More makes more.

Recapping the point, the evidence suggests that leaders must be wise about providing a level of pastoral care that is appropriate in dosage while investing as much energy as possible on activities and abilities that increase the vitality of the church at every scale.

So why can this be so difficult to do? How can something as important as pastoral care become a trap? I believe it is all the short-term feedback loops in a church that reinforce pastoral care (and, for the record, other dissatisfiers like administration, status symbols and titles, and a comfortable environment). If Pastor Jones does not call on member Smith in the hospital prior to surgery, the omission will usually be quickly communicated in an awkward conversation. (Dissatisfiers, like hunger, work fast!) The positive impacts from more important activities may not be as quickly communicated, and sometimes they are hardly communicated at all. This is why a system of collecting organizational intelligence is so important. Organizational intelligence helps a pastor focus on the longer-term, deeper, and more critical impacts of leadership while putting the short-term dissatisfaction in proper perspective.

One prevailing myth about vibrant churches is that many of them are simply kowtowing to the whims of members and that evidence-based approaches only reinforce a consumer mentality. In fact, the evidence shows that such an approach is doomed to failure. When leaders allow their time to be monopolized by reacting to complaints and pandering to the wishes of their members, the chances of their success begin to plummet. (This, however, is not an excuse for leader laziness or arrogance.) Evidence-based discernment helps leaders focus on what needs to be deferred and what must be addressed now. By focusing on the key elements of leadership—developing people, articulating vision, and communicating effectively—leaders stand a much better chance of long-term fruitfulness for the kingdom.

Let us recapitulate the argument to this point.

1. Compared to leaders in other effective organizations today, church leaders have a very poor idea of the perspectives, experiences, and aspirations of the people they are called to lead.
2. Organizational intelligence not only provides leaders with a much clearer understanding of where their congregations are, it opens to them the possibility of an evidence-based discernment process that is biblical and sensible.
3. An evidence-based discernment process represents a spiritual journey that must be undertaken with intentionality and supported by spiritual practice.
4. The target toward which we are aiming is the creation of satisfied (shalom), energized (force of engagement) churches that, given a wide range of options, can positively affect the world for the kingdom of God.
5. Leaders must discipline themselves to focus on the factors that lead to high-satisfaction, high-energy churches as revealed by organizational intelligence in both (a) general patterns discovered across the country and (b) distinct patterns discovered in a particular church.

We now turn our attention to desired outcomes. What do leaders *believe* members want as the outcome of their church activity, and what do members *actually* indicate they want?

Discussion Questions

1. When leaders recruit people in the church, they can either go about it in the easiest way or the most effective way. How effective are the means that your church uses to recruit people to various ministries?

2. In this chapter I identify six things a church must do well to have an energized membership. Conversely, I have never seen a single church that does these six things well that does not have an energized membership.

What do you think would happen in your church in the next three years if your members focused on excelling in those six areas?

3. The organizational intelligence from hundreds of churches indicates that it is more important for a pastor to lead well and preach well than provide great pastoral care. How would your church respond to this type of pastoral leadership?

CHAPTER 7

Getting Clarity about the Destination

Imagine then a fleet or a ship in which there is a captain who is taller and stronger than any of the crew, but he is a little deaf and has a similar infirmity in sight, and his knowledge of navigation is not much better. The sailors are quarrelling with one another about the steering—everyone is of opinion that he has a right to steer, though he has never learned the art of navigation and cannot tell who taught him or when he learned, and will further assert that it cannot be taught, and they are ready to cut in pieces anyone who says the contrary.

—Plato, *The Republic*, Book 6

C larity about where a church is (chaos, recovery, static, transformational) is only part of the organizational intelligence leaders need. Leaders also must have a clear understanding of where members want the church to go. What does forward look like?

Members have a variety of perspectives on the churches they attend as well as a variety of experiences. They also have aspirations and dreams. In their minds, they form an image of the church as they would like to see it. We can assume that members would like their leaders to develop and implement a plan to create the church that they imagine in their minds and hearts.

This mental and emotional image is invisible to the leadership. It cannot be counted like square feet and second graders. Yet, it is essential for leaders in any organization to picture clearly what members would like to see as the desired outcomes of their investment of time, talent, and treasure. Ultimately, members will measure whether the church has succeeded or failed based upon the church as it actually exists overlaid against the mental image they have in their minds. But do leaders know what is in their minds?

The Absence of the Barking Dog

In the Sherlock Holmes story "The Adventure of Silver Blaze," a prize-winning racehorse by that name has mysteriously disappears the night before a big race and his trainer has been murdered. When Inspector Gregory asks, "Is there any point to which you would wish to draw my attention?" Holmes responds, "To the curious incident of the dog in the night-time." But, protests the inspector, "the dog did nothing in the night-time." To which Holmes delivers the punch line: "That was the curious incident."[1]

For Holmes, the absence of barking is the turning point of the case: the dog must have known the intruder. Otherwise, he would have made a fuss. For us in the church, the absence of barking is something that is all too easy to forget.

What is most curious in churches today is the almost total absence of organizational intelligence regarding the perspectives, experiences, and aspirations of the members. It is curious that we do not miss it, perhaps because we do not *know* to miss it. Nowhere is this more evident than when we look at the lack of clarity leaders have regarding the outcomes that are important to members.

In the typical church the primary way leaders try to get in touch with the desired outcomes that members have in mind is through anecdotally-driven processes. In other words, they aggregate the one-on-one conversations they have had with members and combine them with what they have heard and overheard members say in congregational, committee, task force, staff meetings, and so forth, hoping that the result is a good approximation of where the congregation is as a whole. How well does this work?

Twenty-nine leaders of Calvin Presbyterian Church, a large congregation, were asked to indicate how members would prioritize particular congregational activities. (The organizational intelligence for Calvin is found in figure 7.1.) They were asked:

Name of Church:	*Calvin Presbyterian*
Vitality Status:	*Transformational*
Member focus:	*Ministry-focused*
Critical success factors:	*Opportunities for different approaches to decisions*
Level of criticality:	*Low*
Priority Focus:	*Hearth and Home*

Figure 7.1. Calvin Presbyterian Church Organizational Intelligence Profile.
For a definition of terms, please see the glossary in appendix A.

Out of a list of ten priorities, where do you think members overall would rank *"Expand outreach ministries to help people on the margins of society?"*

Please note: We did not ask how leaders would rank this item, which we would expect to vary widely from leader to leader. We asked them how they believe members overall would rank this item, which has only one correct answer. I have chosen this particular question because it seems straightforward and unambiguous in its wording. The following responses represent the actual data. Only the names have been changed.

Peter said members would rank it *first.*
Russ and Sandi said members would rank it *second.*
Tom, Brad, and Betsy said members would rank it *third.*
Bernard, Olive, Sam, and Mary said members would rank it *fourth.*
Lyman, Alice, Zach, and Ted said members would rank it *fifth.*
Linda, Mattie, Carol, David, and Harvey said members would rank it *sixth.*
Cameron, Delilah, Ed, and George said members would rank it *seventh.*
Bill, Andy, Quint, and Rick said members would rank it *next to last.*
Penny said members would rank it *last.*
So what? How important is it to get this right?

If Peter, Russ, Sandi, Tom, Brad, and Betsy are correct, outreach ministries to people living on the margins of society are more important to this congregation than they are for 99 percent of hundreds of mainline churches in our database.2 If they are correct, members in this church are highly motivated to provide direct services to people with a wide range of needs, who might include the homeless, undocumented residents, the unemployed, the addicted, the mentally ill, the prisoners. Strategies to achieve this highest level of engagement might include building alliances with other organizations, forming cell groups of specific populations, even moving worship out of the church building and into other facilities closer to the populations being served and hiring a person to do fund development. If the leadership is able to achieve these outcomes, this will be a church for the textbooks. However, these outcomes will be almost impossible to achieve if Peter, Russ, Sandi, Tom, and Brad are wrong. In fact, if they are wrong, these strategies will generate conflict at nearly every turn.

If Bill, Andy, Quint, Rick, and Penny are correct, outreach ministries to people living on the margins of society are scarcely on the radar for this congregation. If they are correct, members may be highly motivated to achieve other outcomes, which might include reaching new people, developing a comprehensive, lifelong Christian education and formation ministry, and developing a church known for its powerful worship and music. Strategies for achieving any of these are substantially different from those focused on services for people who are marginalized. None of these strategies is likely to work if Bill, Andy, Quint, Rick, and Penny are wrong and they discover in the middle of their plan that outreach ministries actually *are* the highest priority of the congregation.

In the introduction to this book, we saw that leader estimates of the satisfaction and energy levels of a church vary widely from one leader to another, and I asserted that this lack of clarity throws into confusion the entire enterprise of establishing strategy and leadership tasks. In the data we have just reviewed, we see that there is no clarity for leaders regarding the desired outcomes members have in mind for the church. Looking at the estimates for Calvin Presbyterian's outreach priorities that lie on either end, there are at least two radically different churches that leaders have in view. Members in these two churches have very different mental images of desired outcomes, which require markedly different strategies for their realization. In the choice between these two options, a lot is at stake. Which congregation is it? Where does the energy lie in this church? How does a leadership team take any substantial, unified action when their understandings of member aspirations are substantially different from one another? How do leaders preserve any sense of integrity when actions are taken that require they abandon their perceptions of the congregation?

One option for a leadership team is to simply default to the research found in national studies, of which, there are many. Arguably, this has more value than guessing. It begins to open our thinking to evidenced-based approaches. It serves as a potential corrective to some assumptions we may have regarding the larger church that are actually false, and confirms others that we have intuited.

With regard to desired outcomes, members across the country rank a large list of priorities in the order found in figure 7.2.

First	Develop and implement a comprehensive strategy to reach new people and incorporate them into the life of the church.
Second	Make necessary changes to attract families with children and youth to our church.
Third	Move decisively to provide high quality education for every age and stage of life.
Fourth	Develop ministries that work toward healing those broken by life circumstances.
Fifth	Develop the spiritual generosity of the people to financially support the ministry of the church.
Sixth	Strengthen the process by which members are called and equipped for ministry and leadership.
Seventh	Create more opportunities for people to form meaningful relationships (for example, small groups, nurtured friendships, shared meals, etc.).
Eighth	Work to renew and revitalize the community around the church by building coalitions with partners that share this vision and commitment.
Ninth	Expand outreach ministries that provide direct services to those living on the margins of society.
Tenth	Strengthen the management and support of persons in various ministries so that they are able to do what they do best in work that is meaningful and celebrated.
Eleventh	Deepen our sense of connection to God and one another through stronger worship services.
Twelfth	Strengthen the pastoral response of the church in serving people with special needs.
Thirteenth	Work as an advocate for social and institutional change so that society might better reflect the values of the kingdom of God.
Fourteenth	Adapt the opportunities provided by the church, making them more accessible, given the pace and schedule of my life (for example, online education, early morning classes, lunch discussions).
Fifteenth	Change or improve the music of the church to deepen our worship experience.
Sixteenth	Expand the international mission of the church with both financial resources and personal involvement.
Seventeenth	Enlarge or improve the physical facilities of the church to expand or enhance our ministries.

Figure 7.2. Ranked Outcomes for the Typical Mainline Church in the United States[3]

The Advantages and Disadvantages of General Research

When looking at a typical church in the United States, we see that

- reaching new members, especially families with children and youth, is the highest priority.
- developing Christian education and spiritual formation ministries is a very high priority.
- developing ministries of healing is a high priority.
- developing spiritual generosity is a relatively high priority.

Notice, also, that in a typical church in the United States

- members are generally not interested in changing the physical facilities.
- while a small group of folks may be passionate about international mission, it is generally a very low priority for the church as a whole.
- the interest in changing the music in a church is roughly the same as the interest in changing the building. (Changing the hymnal will require roughly the same amount of energy as knocking down a wall!)
- improving pastoral care is a relatively low priority. (We addressed this in the last chapter.)

This kind of general research has value in identifying larger trends and in providing a framework for understanding what is happening in the environment. The problem with such averaged lists and other one-size-fits-all approaches is that they obscure the distinctiveness of particular congregations. One promise of organizational intelligence is that it provides clarity regarding a specific congregation and the outcomes that members envision for their church. For example, when we actually examine the organizational intelligence for individual congregations we discover the following:

- In most churches, enlarging or improving the facilities is the *lowest priority*. But there are some congregations where it is the *highest priority*.
- In one church, attracting families with children and youth is the *highest priority*. In another church, attracting families with children and youth is the *lowest priority*.
- In one church, healing people broken by life circumstances is the *highest priority*. In another church, healing people broken by life circumstances is the *lowest priority*.
- In one church, working to renew and revitalize the community around the church is the *highest priority*. In another church, working to renew and revitalize the community around the church is the *lowest priority*.
- In one church, providing opportunities for members to form relationships is the *second highest priority*. In another church, providing opportunities for members to form relationships is the *lowest priority*.

We now see one reason why the plethora of books on the market aimed at renewing and growing local congregations fail to have the impact their authors envisioned. Churches not only have different starting points but their members have different mental images of the outcomes they envision for their churches, and, as we have seen, anecdotally-driven, storytelling processes do not give leaders a clear understanding of the people they lead.

In fact, we often learn the most not by looking at what a church shares in common with other churches but by discovering what is distinctive about it. We have already seen that what is distinctive about transformational churches is not their size, setting, theological perspective, personal piety, or pastoral care. What is distinctive about transformational churches is their worship experience, flexibility, commitment to lifelong learning, adaptable programming, quality relationships, and open governance system.

Members of transformational churches also have a distinct set of outcomes in mind when they envision the church. Some of the outcomes are the same as other churches; church growth, for example, appears at the top of nearly every list. But members in transformational churches tend to be more externally focused on international mission, services to the marginalized, and advocacy for social change.

For congregations seeking a pathway out of chaos, recovery, or apathy, it is often what is distinctive about them that offers the best clues for moving forward. I have in front of me the organizational intelligence for a church deep in the recovery quadrant. The priorities listed by their members are consistent with what you would find in thousands of churches across the country with two exceptions: First, in the typical church, deepening the worship experience is the eleventh priority. For the members of the church before me it is fourth. Second, in the typical church, developing spiritual generosity is fifth priority. For the members of the church before me it is twelfth priority.

If we knew nothing else about this church, these two pieces of organizational intelligence provide us with a wealth of insight into the image of the church that resides in the minds of members. As a whole, they envision a worship experience that more powerfully connects them to God and one another. They also envision a church that is not so focused on giving that it eclipses the other aspects of the church's life and ministry. The capacity of the leadership, in partnership with the congregation, to achieve these outcomes will have a significant impact on how well this church recovers.

So here is the question: Would a group of twenty-nine leaders in this church be able to come to this same conclusion when some leaders believe that improving worship is the congregation's highest priority, some think it is members' second priority, some think it is members' third priority, some, the fourth priority, some, the fifth priority, some, the sixth priority, some, the seventh, some, the eighth, some, the ninth, and some think it is the congregation's lowest priority? Yet most leaders will enter into important discernment processes with major consequences for the future of their church without the organizational intelligence that would project onto a single screen the same picture for every leader. There is no fault here. It is impossible to miss what you have never had. It is easy to overlook the dog that is not barking.

Generational Intelligence

If it is difficult for leaders to estimate member priorities as a whole, it is well-nigh impossible for them to parse those by generational cohort. For churches anxious to reach families with children and youth, clarity regarding those differences is critical.

First	Develop and implement a comprehensive strategy to reach new people.
Second	Make necessary changes to attract families with children and youth to our church.
Third	Develop the spiritual generosity of the people to financially support the ministry of the church.
Fourth	Develop ministries that work toward healing those broken by life circumstances.
Fifth	Move decisively to provide high quality education for every age and stage of life.

Figure 7.3. Ranked Outcomes for the Traditionalists in a Study of 30 Churches[4]

Figure 7.3 shows the results from a study of thirty churches that indicates the priorities for Traditionalists (over age sixty-five). In figure 7.4 the priorities for Millennials (under age thirty-five) contain both similarities and differences. Notice the three priorities that are shared by both groups.

- Develop and implement a comprehensive strategy to reach new people.
- Make necessary changes to attract families with children and youth to our church.
- Move decisively to provide high quality education for every age and stage of life.

Members at both ends of the generation spectrum believe that it is important for the church to reach others, especially families with children and youth, and to provide ministries that educate and form them. These shared priorities establish some common ground for folks that have had such different experiences of the world.

First	Make necessary changes to attract families with children and youth to our church.
Second	Expand outreach ministries that provide direct services to those living on the margins of society.
Third	Move decisively to provide high quality education for every age and stage of life.
Fourth	Develop and implement a comprehensive strategy to reach new people.
Fifth	Create more opportunities for people to form meaningful relationships.

Figure 7.4. Ranked Outcomes for the Millennials in a Study of 30 Churches

However, the differences between these two groups are equally noteworthy: Traditionalists are concerned about developing the spiritual generosity of members. They are often carrying the lion's share of the church budget and they are anxious regarding the church's financial future after they are gone. Millennials, on the other hand do not connect with the traditional language of stewardship, though they have other ways of expressing generosity. This can be a challenge in a church when the concepts and language that elicit a response in one generation actually impede the engagement of another. Traditionalists are also more concerned for the healing ministry of the church. Given the fact that longer lifespans have resulted in chronic health issues in the later years of life, Traditionalists want the church to have these concerns in view.

Millennials are more focused on community and global impact, which is reflected in their second priority but does not appear as a priority for Traditionalists. They are also concerned that the churches provide avenues for building relationships. Traditionalists are at a stage of life where those networks are often in place.

These general findings are useful for churches in discernment processes that are trying to design ministries with cross-generational appeal. The deeper lesson is that leaders need organizational intelligence that enables them to parse the aspirations of different groups within the church so that the shared and distinct priorities and perspectives in each generational group can be honored.

How are leaders to deal with these outcomes that members indicate are important to them? Do they simply accept these priority lists at face value and build them into a plan? What happens when members of a congregation indicate they want two things that are at odds with one another?

We turn to the subject of dissonance in the next chapter.

Discussion Questions

1. This chapter revisits the fact that leaders have wide-ranging guesses about the thinking of members, this time regarding the aspirations of members for the future of the church. How difficult does this make it for a leader to discern what direction the church should go? Do you think it is possible to motivate members over the long term to go in a direction that does not interest them?

2. Figure 7.2 lists the priorities for members in a typical church in the United States. However, this can vary a great deal from one church to another. How close would your church members' aspirations for the future be to those of a typical church? How certain are you about the answer?

3. Members under thirty-five years of age often have very different priorities from members over sixty-five. In your church would you say that you (1) try to accommodate those differences, (2) ignore those differences, or (3) are largely unaware of the differences?

CHAPTER 8

Spiritual Dissonance

I have three walnuts, and each one of them wants two.
—President Abraham Lincoln, 1809-1865,
explaining why his children were quarreling

You can have anything you want, but not everything you want.
—Peter McWilliams, *Life 101*, 1997

S hortly after completing the manuscript for a previous book, *The Fly in the Ointment: Why Denominations Aren't Helping Their Congregations, and How They Can*, I sent it to my friend Dr. James Mead for his input. Jim is a gifted preacher and served as the executive pastor of the Pittsburgh Presbytery. He called me on the phone and said, "I like the book, but I disagree with you on one point. I do not believe that churches *really* want help to become vital, growing congregations even though they say that they do."

In support of his point, I will share the true story of two churches that I will call First Church and Second Church. The organizational intelligence for First Church is found in figure 8.1. The organizational intelligence for Second Church is found in figure 8.2.

Both First Church and Second Church are members of the same denomination and serve basically the same community, one almost entirely made up of older adults. First Church is thriving with hundreds of people in worship and multiple ministries that serve the members, the community, and the world. Second Church is bumping along with about twenty people in worship.

When I looked at the organizational intelligence coming back from these two churches (not included in the charts below), I was struck by the fact that the highest priority for the members of Second Church is reaching families with children and youth, even though the community has virtually no families with children and youth. This is given the lowest priority by the members of First Church . . . which is thriving.

Name of Church:	*First Church*
Vitality Status:	*Transformational*
Member focus:	*Ministry-focused*
Critical success factors:	*How spiritual experiences impact member perspectives*
Level of criticality:	*Very low*
Priority Focus:	*Performance*

Figure 8.1. First Church Organizational Intelligence Profile.
For a definition of terms, please see the glossary in appendix A.

Name of Church:	*Second Church*
Vitality Status:	*Recovery*
Member focus:	*Clergy-focused*
Critical success factors:	*Adapting worship to meet the needs of the community*
Level of criticality:	*High*
Priority Focus:	*Hearth and Home*

Figure 8.2. Second Church Organizational Intelligence Profile.
For a definition of terms, please see the glossary in appendix A.

Three Types of Dissonance

What Second Church exhibits is a type of dissonance. Webster defines *dissonance* as inconsistency between the beliefs one holds or between one's actions and one's beliefs. Scaled up to the level of a congregation, I define *dissonance* as wanting two different things that are mutually exclusive. As we shall see later in the chapter, this dissonance is usually sustained by a disconnect between faith and action, which makes it a spiritual issue as well.

For this reason, I call it *spiritual dissonance,* which I define as a state in which a congregation desires two different things that are mutually exclusive and that is sustained by a disconnect between faith and action.

Spiritual dissonance is at the heart of the suffering for many churches, and it manifests itself in a number of different ways. The first is *contextual dissonance,* which is a contradiction between a congregation's priorities and the needs of the community it feels called to serve. The church we have been learning about (and from), Second Church, wanted (1) a ministry with children and youth (2) in a community without children and youth. These two realities are contradictory. The contradiction is sustained by the church's stated mission to reach and serve its community and the actions of the church that essentially ignore the people who live in the community. As a result, Second Church is struggling. (I urge you not to jump too quickly into judgment of this small church. To one degree or another, we all have our contradictions that hamper our spiritual walk.)

Organizational intelligence surfaces contextual dissonance by providing a mechanism through which members express their priorities for investing energy and resources. Armed with that clarity, leaders can then overlay the priorities of the congregation with other information that describes the community the church feels called to reach. Leaders in other churches often discover that the community context described for First Church and Second Church is becoming more common across the country—that is, decreasing numbers of families with children and increasing numbers of older adults.

A second type of spiritual dissonance is strategic-tactical. *Strategic-tactical dissonance* is wanting to get to a destination (strategic) without having to take the required journey (tactics). Concretely, this means that members may want their church to grow, to become vital, energized, effective, transformative (all long-term, strategic goals) without making the required changes in what they do or how they do it (short-term, tactical steps). During my years as the pastor of a small, family-sized church that grew to become a pastoral-sized church, and then a program-sized church, I came to believe that many churches remain small because they resist the choices required to grow. Adding a second service in a small church (a tactic), for example, is often key to growth (a strategy), but it's mightily resisted because it "splits the family."

Strategic-tactical dissonance can surface around issues of generosity. For example, Rev. James Steen, who led St. Paul and Our Redeemer Episcopal Church in Chicago through a significant period of growth and renewal, began by hiring a staff person for family ministries. Such a step requires additional funding, usually generated by increased giving from members. Generosity is a spiritual issue, one where a disconnect between faith and action can be easy to ignore. When the organizational intelligence from a church indicates that spiritual generosity is a relatively low priority for members, even though the average giving is only 1.4 percent of the household income (which is very low), a clear dissonance is surfaced between the strategic goal of reaching families and the steps required to achieve that goal. Organizational intelligence can be powerful in bringing strategic-tactical dissonance into bold relief.

Strategic-tactical dissonance can take many forms. Other examples would include the following:

- The need for a membership trained to engage people in their network of relationships but the members' lack of motivation for training.
- The need for substantial change to reach a diverse ethnic community but the church's lack of flexibility.
- The need for a pastor who is invests time and energy to affect the external community, but the membership's high demand for pastoral care.
- The need for a church to move toward a Web-based marketing approach, but a resistance to information technology.

Organizational intelligence can surface each of these examples of strategic-tactical dissonance.

A third type of spiritual dissonance is *interpersonal-corporate dissonance*, which is wanting a vital congregation while engaging in interpersonal behaviors that are unhealthy. In organizational intelligence, this type of dissonance often manifests itself around issues of conflict.

When the church is at its best, interpersonal-corporate dissonance issues that are surfaced by organizational intelligence can be addressed using the spiritual resources available to us as Christians. Bill Johnston, a now retired Episcopal priest, worked for a number of years helping churches understand and appreciate the benefits of organizational intelligence in their ministries. He tells the story of one church that engaged in an assessment process. The organizational intelligence that was generated disclosed an unusually high level of conflict. He brought the report to the congregation in the context of his sermon. During the passing of the peace, he gave instructions that departed from the customary "The peace of the Lord be with you," "And also with you." Instead he asked members to say to one another, "I was wrong. Would you please forgive me?" "Yes, I forgive you." The effect was electric.

In cases of interpersonal-corporate dissonance, the spiritual resources of the church are often unavailable, sometimes because of a dissonance between liturgy and life. In our liturgy we confess our sins (admit we have been wrong and ask to be forgiven), receive forgiveness (decide to stop punishing ourselves), and pass the peace (decide to stop punishing others). What a strategic resource this would be for a church if it could practice this with regard to the contradictory impulses exhibited in congregations! Unfortunately, the resources of our liturgy are often not available to us, not because we fail to live up to their standard but because we deem them to be impractical or even impossible.

Name of Church:	*Living Waters Church*
Vitality Status:	*Recovery*
Member focus:	*Ministry-focused*
Critical success factors:	*Disturbing level of conflict*
	Resolve problems through mutual effort
Level of criticality:	*High*
Priority Focus:	*Hearth and Home*

Figure 8.3. Living Waters Church Organizational Intelligence Profile.
For a definition of terms, please see the glossary in appendix A.

In figure 8.3, you will find the organizational intelligence for Living Waters Church, revealing a congregation where the critical success factors for its vitality are focused on conflict resolution. The board asked me to lead a workshop for the leadership team. In one exercise I asked them to practice saying to one another, "I was wrong, will you please forgive me." In the middle of the exercise a woman raised her hand and asked, "Don't you think that it is really impossible for some people in the church to say this?" Spiritually, the root of the conflict was laid bare by that great question.

When members of a congregation cannot seek and receive forgiveness from one another, they have been robbed of a potent resource. The penicillin vial is empty; the infection of pride and resentment grows unchecked. We are left with the cry of Jeremiah 8:22, "Is there no balm in Gilead? Is there no physician there? Why then is there no healing for the wound of my people?" While being able to ask forgiveness certainly doesn't guarantee success in conflict resolution, the inability to do so almost certainly guarantees its failure. What is important is that it was organizational intelligence that helped disclose the dissonance that had them stymied. (The good news is that the church *was* able to resolve this dissonance and enter into a sustained period of healing and renewal.)

The Purpose of Organizational Intelligence: A Window in the Wall

None of these examples may be new or particularly insightful for seasoned church leaders. However, the three types of dissonance described above are often invisible to the church as a whole, and invisible even to many members of the leadership team.

I am writing this chapter in a beautiful home situated by the Pedernales River just west of Austin, Texas. The house was built by an artist. As one would expect, it is well appointed with art of every description—paintings, sculpture, pottery, and tapestry. This particular artist wanted the guest to experience more than what was hanging on the walls; she wanted the guest to experience the invisible. Just outside the patio door, she installed a round window in the stucco where you can see the straw, black marble, and feathers that the wall is made of. She wants you to see the art that is visible *on* the walls, but she also wants you to see *into* the walls, into that which is all around you but would otherwise be invisible.

Organizational intelligence provides a window into the invisible patterns of a congregation, revealing both the gifts and the shadows that sabotage a church's best efforts. Sometimes leaders will look at the organizational intelligence from their congregation and exclaim, "This can't be right. It is contradictory." I try to be silent and just let that thought sink in. Often, after a few seconds of silence, another leader will respond, "Maybe that's because we *are* contradictory."

Why It Is Important to Deal with Spiritual Dissonance

I hope that it is now becoming clear why it is important to identify and deal with spiritual dissonance.

Spiritual dissonance invisibly impedes the progress of a church toward the goals its members believe are important. Once while I was racing across a lake near Nakina, Canada, on a borrowed boat, I hit a rock just below the surface and broke the boat's propeller. The rock hadn't been on any of the maps I had. Spiritual dissonance is like that invisible rock. Organizational intelligence can help a church steer around it.

Spiritual dissonance causes church to call the wrong leaders. Pastors are often given one picture of the church by a call committee (one side of the contradiction), only to get on board and discover that what the church also wants is someone else (the other side of the contradiction).

Spiritual dissonance burns out leaders. Since spiritual dissonance has contradictory desires, it almost always results in contradictory expectations of leaders, both clergy and lay. Failure on one side or another is guaranteed.

Spiritual dissonance separates faith from action, which diminishes both faith and action. I was in an evangelism workshop led by Dr. Ron Rand, who said, "Faith without works is like a spirit without a body. That's a ghost. Works without faith is like a body without a spirit. That's a corpse."

Steps in Dealing with Spiritual Dissonance

So, once the organizational intelligence discloses spiritual dissonance, how does a church deal with it?

First, leaders and members need to give a name to what they are experiencing: *spiritual dissonance.* Naming gives people a sense of power and control. It also shifts the conversation to the right topic. The problem is not simply the pastor or the elders or the programs or the location. The problem is that the congregation as a whole wants two things that are contradictory.

Second, it is important to realize that other churches have found their way through this spiritual dissonance and there is no reason any particular church cannot as well. The fact that other churches have succeeded at this is not an indication that they are better or smarter. Often it is simply that they have found a way to escape from the prison in which their minds have confined them.

Third, it helps to recognize that spiritual dissonance is indeed a spiritual issue. By trying to serve two conflicting masters, to use a biblical image, a church ends up generating intense and conflicting emotions that arrest spiritual progress. One effect of spiritual dissonance is that members often misread what is really going on. For the members who care, the church feels stuck. It is easy for them to conclude that there is something fundamentally wrong with the church, with its leadership, or with the community itself. This is compounded by the erroneous belief that a *real* church is one that has families with children and youth, which was the situation at Second Church.

To appreciate how this dissonance obscures the issue, let's go back to First Church and Second Church and compare how a church that has resolved this dissonance sees things. When its ministry to reach families and youth does not bear fruit, it recognizes that it is not anyone's fault. It goes back to its core purpose, which is to make disciples, and considers how it might make disciples in the community that is actually present: older adults. When someone suggests that the church convert some of the space it once used for youth ministry into a screening room for the parish nurse, members may be tempted to fall back into the erroneous belief that they are failing, which conjures nostalgia, guilt, shame, and even anger. But armed with the truth, they remind themselves of their core purpose and that a ministry with and for older adults is every bit as valid as a ministry with children.

If this is indeed a spiritual issue, then it must be addressed with spiritual resources. In reflecting upon this tendency to give residence to thoughts that are false and contradictory to God's purpose, I find it helpful to understand it as a characteristic of an evil assault, as described in the eighth chapter of the Gospel of John. There, Jesus described Satan as a murderer, but with a particularly insidious method of killing: he is a liar. Lies that are held as truth have a singular lethality, because they can be buttressed with the same fortifications that we use to guard our highest ideals. The belief that a church without children is not a church is often held with the same intensity and tenacity as the belief in love and justice.

All the same, it is a lie nonetheless. These lies undergirding spiritual dissonance are no trifle. They have the power to destroy individuals and spiritual communities alike. They hamstring the ministries of churches for years. The good news, yes, the *good news*, is that the church has the resources to deal with spiritual issues.

Here is where I differ with many of my colleagues in the field of church development. The issues are not simply those of strategy and tactics. Nor are they simply matters of low self-esteem or the need for affirmation and appreciation. Rather, these are spiritual issues. They go back to the vows of our baptism and confession: the renouncing of evil and its power in the world; the confession of complicity, conscious and unconscious; the acceptance of forgiveness; the offering of peace; and the joyful resolve to live a new life.

This leads to the fourth step in dealing with spiritual dissonance: take concrete action. Churches dealing with spiritual dissonance need opportunities to experiment with small, concrete steps and to then watch what happens. If a church in an older adult community discerns that it must affirm the truth and value of that ministry, it needs to be given short-term, concrete opportunities to actually try it. Sponsor an outing for the independent living population at a local retirement center. Serve refreshments at an existing function in the community. Find a list of recently retired folks in the community and take them to lunch. Try to let go of the expectation of recruiting members to the church. Care for them, listen to them, and share the congregation's story. Then see what happens.

Perhaps this is the place to emphasize that the positive, constructive, and vigorous engagement of members is essential to dealing with spiritual dissonance successfully. Since the spiritual dissonance in a church is not located in any single individual but in the entire system, the entire system must shift. Churches with spiritual dissonance often fall prey to the temptation of blaming an individual or small group when the contradictions within the system lead to a repeated pattern of failure.

The reality is that a critical mass of members must understand their responsibility to address the issue and commit to real changes in their behavior that can bring the energies of the church into alignment. The leaders' task is to communicate clearly what members are being asked to do. Organizational intelligence is critical to this enterprise, because it helps members understand *why* changes are required. Leaders may get compliance from a few members using a "Because I said so" approach, but to achieve real and lasting changes that are hard-wired in the system requires that members understand clearly what they are being asked to do and why. Organizational intelligence provides the *why*.

As a fifth step, churches beginning to move out of spiritual dissonance need to romance the journey. Celebrate the presence and working of the Spirit in new endeavors. Tell stories. Offer prayers of gratitude. Recite the faithfulness of God.

Let me share how I, as the president of Holy Cow! Consulting, have tried to contribute to this celebration and romancing the journey. When I have discovered a church that has become transformational, I have sent the pastor and governing board a letter indicating that Holy Cow! Consulting has declared their church a Transformational Congregation. With their permission, I then send a press release to the local newspaper, their middle judicatory, and their national denominational publication. I conduct a webinar with the pastor and a lay leader and I invite everyone on my mailing list to participate and hear how the congregation became transformational. Finally, I ask the leaders of the congregation to make themselves available as mentors to leadership teams in other churches.

In those cases where a church has made a significant journey from recovery to transformation, I have also hired a writer to interview church leaders, and I post the story on my website. Organizational intelligence not only makes visible the shadows of dissonance that must be overcome but it also reveals what is beautiful inside our walls—the golden straw, the black marble, and the feathers of flight. Just as what impedes a church is invisible, what makes for its renewal is often invisible as well—the tough choices, the small repentances, the moments of forgiveness, and the acts of peace. Organizational intelligence helps us know what we have to celebrate.

Regression Is Normal

Finally, accept the fact that as a church begins to move out of spiritual dissonance regression is normal. Members will be tempted to go back to self-defeating patterns of thinking. Here is something that may help. In advance of taking any step, identify those situations in which members will be most vulnerable and include some of the reasons people might give for not following through with the small, concrete steps they decided to take (step four above). Here are some possibilities:

- It won't make any difference anyway.
- I remember when we had thirty kids in the confirmation class. How many children do we have now?
- Older adults don't have spiritual needs. They have been in the church for years.
- I don't have anything to give.

Churches have to be prepared to address those kinds of responses *before* they arise so that members are not caught off guard by them. Other churches that have successfully navigated a similar transition can help by serving as sources of inspiration and practical advice.

Is Organizational Intelligence a Substitute for Listening to God?

We are now prepared to answer the question, Doesn't a focus on organizational intelligence become a substitute for listening to God? It is a fact of our human condition that anything can become a substitute for listening to God. However, generally the opposite is the case. Organizational intelligence surfaces issues that cannot be dealt with through political polls, majority votes, facilitated processes, or data analysis. The issues that surface require the resources of the gospel. In fact, the widespread reticence across the church for its leaders to get clarity regarding the state of their churches and their ministries is not an affirmation of grace; it is an indication that we do not fully trust it.

Theologian Helmut Thielicke proposes that human beings' basic controversy with God does not take the form of what he calls "explosions of Promethean defiance," where we shake a fist in God's face and refuse to do what God is asking. Instead it settles into a deep impulse in which self-diagnosis is hampered by the heart that tries to defend itself. "When God suddenly takes my side in the form of Jesus Christ and justifies me in relationship to his own claim, I am encircled by this peace and liberated from the power that forced me to avoid self-awareness."[1] When we trust the grace of God, we discover that we do not need to fear the information that organizational intelligence offers us, even when it discloses areas in which a congregation is beset by contradictions and behaves as its own worst enemy. Or as John Calvin put it, "Indeed, our very poverty better discloses the infinitude of benefits reposing in God. The miserable ruin, into which the rebellion of the first man cast us especially compels us to look upward."[2] Self-awareness drives us deeper into the reality of grace (as opposed to the idea of grace), and grace draws out the poison of wounded pride aroused by the darts of self-awareness (as opposed to the idea of self-awareness).

I have mentioned a couple of specific instances of spiritual dissonance that are identified by organizational intelligence, but these examples are offered only to illustrate a more general problem. There are others.

Organizational intelligence does not guarantee that a church will engage the spiritual resources that will make for its liberation from the spiritual dissonance that it discloses. However, organizational intelligence offers churches a chance to make a fresh set of conscious choices from renewed minds rather than travel down the unconscious, rutted patterns that, though they may start in different new places, will end up at the same destinations.

Corporate Pastoral Care

We have seen how organizational intelligence can help a congregation identify the spiritual dissonance that is hampering their journey. In addition, we have seen how spiritual dissonance can take a toll on pastors and other leaders who are thrust into a no-win situation. There is another perspective to consider. Without organizational intelligence, leaders often fail the most fundamental principle of Christian leadership: beginning where people are.

Most folks in the pastorate today were required to engage in a significant training experience called clinical pastoral education. Thrown into profound individual and family experiences of life and loss, hope and heartbreak, students learn how to minister in a cross-disciplinary environment, to explore their own responses through written verbatims and group supervision, but most of all, to be fully present to a person rather than ladening the person with their own expectations.

Pastors receive virtually no training in how to provide pastoral care to a congregation as a whole. Churches can be every bit as traumatized or paralyzed by the spiritual state of their existence as a person wrestling with cancer. Yet there is nothing approaching the thoroughness of a clinical pastoral education experience to deal with this collective spiritual crisis that has no surgical gown to signal its presence. In a hospital, a student learns to work cross-professionally with an array of people, technologies, and practices, integrating not only the spiritual, the physical, and the emotional but also the medical, the nuclear, the social, the informational, the legal, and the financial. Yet, when it comes to understanding where the people of the church are as a whole, the pastor has almost no training on how to integrate information technology, mathematics, or research tools into the spiritual palette of resources. On the contrary, for many pastors these tools represent a capitulation to the secular, treating the church as a business rather than a spiritual enterprise, and so they reject them.

Organizational intelligence is a means of providing a more integrated and better equipped pastoral care to the church as a whole. It is a way that leaders can fulfill the challenging command in the book of James (1:19): "Be quick to listen, slow to speak." Pastors have ample opportunities to speak and multiple occasions to listen to individuals. Beyond the dreaded annual congregational meeting, they have almost no way to listen to the perspectives, experiences, and aspirations of their people as a whole. I never fail to be moved by the words of Matthew 9:36. "When [Jesus] saw the crowds, he had compassion on them, because they were harassed and helpless, like sheep without a shepherd." Most of Paul's letters were not written to individuals but to entire churches, and in many cases it does not take much reading between the lines to discern that Paul is trying to get a read on where the church is as a whole.

It is difficult to lead a congregation to a new place if we do not know the starting point. If I am in a strange city and call a pastor who I am scheduled to visit and ask for directions, the first question I am going to be asked is "Where are you now?" If I do not know, that pastor cannot help me, no matter how well he or she may know the city. In the same way, a pastor will find it difficult to lead a church to achieve a vision without first knowing where the church is.

Leading a church requires being in sync with them. It is something like catching a fish. If you pull too hard, the line will break and you will lose the fish. If you don't pull at all, the fish spits the hook and you lose the fish.

I remember starting at my second church and attending worship and music committee meetings where the chairperson always began his opening prayers with the words, "Lord, none of us wants to be here tonight." Now this was a good man and I enjoyed his company, but his soul seemed to have been shaped by a leadership style that demanded nothing of people, and so they were becoming nothing. But how do I know for sure? Is this just one soul's malaise? Or is he a hologram of the entire system? In leading the church do I let up on the line? Or do I pull harder to move them forward? Without organizational intelligence, pastors are often too close to really know.

Trinity Church is a large mainline congregation in the upper Midwest. To look at it, you would think it was flourishing. A new wing was just added to the church and no expense was spared in its construction and furnishings. The music in the worship service is little short of spectacular. The organizational intelligence from the church reveals a different picture. (See figure 8.4.) The church has become what I refer to as a stadium church, with a few people engaged in ministry but most watching from the stands. The members in 95 percent of the churches in our database of mainline churches feel more engaged in ministry than they do at Trinity. What happened?

Name of Church:	*Trinity Church*
Vitality Status:	*Recovery*
Member focus:	*Ministry-focused*
Critical success factors:	*Opportunities for pastor and lay to lead worship together*
	The pastor's articulation of a vision for the future
Level of criticality:	*High*
Priority Focus:	*Paraclete*

Figure 8.4. Trinity Church Organizational Intelligence Profile.
For a definition of terms, please see the glossary in appendix A.

The current pastor accepted the call to come to the church about ten years ago. He is a talented man, loves the church, . . . and is also independently wealthy. He personally paid for most of the building addition. His annual financial contribution makes up two-thirds of the church's budget. Over time, church members have collectively taken less and less responsibility for ministry. As with any system fortunate enough to have a very gifted person, the church has become crippled by its own dependency. Here is the point: What was happening to the church as a whole at Trinity was not caused by a failure of love. Rather, the pastor did not have the organizational intelligence that would have indicated he was asking too little of his people. There was just too much slack in the line.

We are called to be fishers of people. Organizational intelligence is one way we collectively know how to hold our people on the line, not too tightly but also not too gently, so that we all end up in the boat and finish our journey together.

In the next chapter we will take a deeper look at the organizational side of dissonance by examining the various operating systems in churches that organizational intelligence can reveal.

Discussion Questions

1. Can you think of a time in your life when you wanted two things that were mutually exclusive and you couldn't bring yourself to choose one option over the other? What makes it hard to admit this? Can you think of a situation where a church might have a similar struggle?

2. Are there any ways that your church might be experiencing spiritual dissonance? If so, what makes it difficult to address these situations of dissonance?

3. Do you believe that your church asks too little or too much of your members? How can you know for sure?

CHAPTER 9

Operating Systems

*Never ask what sort of computer a guy drives. If he's a
Mac user, he'll tell you. If not, why embarrass him?*
—Tom Clancy, *Escape the Pace*, 2002

I have been working in the field of organizational intelligence with churches
and regional bodies in one role or another for more than thirty years.
For most of those years I have used a program called SPSS (Statistical
Package for the Social Sciences) to process information from those thousands
of assessments. Of course, there were no Windows platforms when it first
came out; it is a DOS program. That has not been a problem. Until now. The
program will not work on the computer I just purchased. There is nothing
wrong with the program itself. It simply will not run on the operating system
of my new computer. All I get are error messages.

Every Church Has an Operating System

Like computers, every church has an operating system. (I use the term
operating system interchangeably with *organizational culture*.) The system is
composed of what it deems important, the variety of ways it communicates
and reinforces those values, and the penalties it imposes if those values are
violated. It is relatively easy to determine which operating system is running on

a computer. It is more difficult to figure out the operating system in a church. Nonetheless, it is critical to any significant discernment process that leaders do so. Why is this so important? Many great plans and programs that might work elsewhere may not run well in a particular church's operating system without generating a lot of error messages!

Growth strategies require . . .	But the operating system values . . .	Blue Screen Error messages
new groups for new people	new people to help rejuvenate old groups	***Major Error*** Long-time teachers and group leaders make appointments to see the pastor.
low entry thresholds into church activities (including worship)	complexity and familiarity	***Major Error*** Conflict over music, screens, hymn-books, pews
faith sharing	faith thinking and feeling	***Major Error*** We are not Jehovah's Witnesses.
body of Christ	family	***Major Error*** Our church doesn't feel like a family anymore.

Figure 9.1. Operating Systems and Error Messages

In 95 percent of the churches we assess, members indicate their highest priority is reaching new members.[1] In most churches, the strategies required to actually accomplish numeric growth will not run very well on the local operating system. Some examples are found in figure 9.1, "Operating Systems and Error Messages." The first column refers to approaches that are often required for growth, for example, "new groups for new people." This is because the relational networks and patterns in established groups are already set. They also have a shared history that newcomers have not experienced. Newcomers entering those groups often have trouble fitting in and either never get established or drop out after a short period of time.

The system, however, does not value the creation of new groups (second column in figure 9.1). It values existing groups and wants new people to help keep them going. Members of long-established groups interpret the reticence of a pastor to channel new members their way as a lack of support and appreciation of their history, especially as members die, become homebound, or move away. The fact that the pastor has violated the operating system, creates an error message in the form of members' visits, phone calls, and emails to the pastor expressing their concern that he or she cares only for the new people (third column in figure 9.1). Blue screen error messages are the most serious kind.

There is nothing new here. Every seasoned pastor has experienced the consequences of trying to run a church-growth strategy in a church with core values that are maintenance-based. Every middle judicatory staff person has dealt with it. Every church consultant can spot it. What, then, makes this so difficult to deal with? There are many factors, but one is simple. It is known as the problem of the expert.

The Problem of the Expert

The problem of the expert is one that emerges most readily in our experience of the legal system. How much weight do we give an expert's opinion when a person's freedom (or life) is at stake? How much control do we give away and simply capitulate to the thinking of the expert who will tell us the answer? It is not an issue we encounter only in a courtroom. The truth is that most people do not want an expert to simply give them the answer when anything significant is on the line. Churches are no different.

Jesus both knew and practiced this. He taught using parables. A parable is a puzzle that the listener must solve by unfolding it. That's why preachers love parables; they lend themselves to a process of narrative unfolding. The experience of "getting" a parable is very similar to solving any other puzzle. Once you solve it, the solution belongs to you. There is a power granted to the hearer of a parable. No one can take the answer away, because no one gave it to the hearer in the first place. Ultimately, it is not a matter of what you have heard, it is a matter of the state of your ears and their ability to solve what you have heard. "Whoever has ears, let them hear" (Matt. 11:15).

I have found that most churches do not want an expert. What they want is a specialist. A specialist is a person who does not necessarily *know* the answer but can help someone *find* the answer. Contrast the surgeon that delivers the news that you do not have cancer and simply asks you to believe her as the expert with a second surgeon who walks you through the results of the physical examination, the blood work, and the CAT scan. The first is functioning as an expert, the second as a specialist. Which one is more compelling, more reassuring?

Organizational Intelligence and the Conversion from Experts to Specialists

Organizational intelligence is the CAT scan that turns the pastor, the lay leader, the consultant, or the judicatory staff person into a specialist instead of an expert. Organizational intelligence is simply a mirror reflecting back what members have said so that those who are trying to lead or support a congregation are not butting members head to head with their expert opinion. They are putting the X-ray up on the wall and then moving to the congregation's side. Theologically, this shift to the side of the congregation is the movement from law to grace, from judge to paraclete. Psychologically, it is a shift from parent to sibling from dependency to responsibility.

Congregations are best equipped to identify and take seriously the operating system of their church if they discover it in their own witness rather than being told it by an expert. This is one of the promising aspects of organizational intelligence. Used properly, it can help congregations discover the self-defeating behaviors that have them stuck and to understand the error messages that keep popping up in spite of their best efforts. Insight does not guarantee liberation, but the lack of insight almost always guarantees defeat.

Two Key Factors in a Church Operating System

There are, of course, many different aspects to the operating system of a church. I have found two that are key: theological perspective and flexibility.

I am aware that there are many different ways to parse *theological perspective*. No matter where I go, I seem to find a way to offend someone with some nuance of language or another. Some would claim that evangelical and conservative are different. Others would assert that liberal and progressive are not the same. After one presentation, a member stopped me in the middle of a restroom door to tell me that I was offending him by the use of the word *progressive*. Suffice it to say there is a large degree of diversity of theological perspectives in the United States. On a statement regarding biblical inerrancy that includes not only faith but also science and history, I have some churches where 90 percent of members clearly agree with the statement and other churches where only 5 percent clearly agree.

Flexibility is something altogether different from theological perspective. It describes the preference of a church regarding change. Some churches like to discover patterns that work and stick with them. We call these *settled churches*. Others prefer more novelty. We call these adaptable churches. Again, people may disagree about how best to talk about flexibility (and how much is the right amount), but we can certainly agree that there is a high level of diversity as we examine the organizational intelligence of one church compared to another. For example, on the issue of welcoming change in worship, I see churches where only 10 percent of members clearly agree that they welcome change, while in other churches it is 80 percent or higher. These churches are just as different from one another as the churches at the opposite ends of the theological spectrum mentioned in the paragraph above.

The organizational intelligence from a wide range of churches indicates that there are four different types of operating systems in churches.

Conservative-settled
Progressive-settled
Progressive-adaptable
Conservative-adaptable

I have discovered over the years that these four church types have strikingly different operating systems, that is, values and behaviors that they support or penalize. They each have characteristic strengths and they each have a shadow side; that is, an area where they resist the very things they need most for health and vitality. If they do not find ways to deal effectively with the shadow side of their community, it will sabotage their best efforts. These four systems, and their shadow sides, are described in the pages that follow.

Conservative-Settled Operating Systems: Hearth and Home

I refer to churches in the conservative-settled quadrant as Hearth and Home systems. Hearth and Home churches are ultimately concerned with a clearly defined faith that is lived out in a community valuing structure and stability. At their best, these cultures serve as guardians of hard-won understandings and time-honored traditions. They offer a measure of shelter from the frenetic pace of change in the world. In their outreach to others, they not only invite them into faith but also to "come home" to a faith community that has all the expectations and rewards of a family. It is common in Hearth and Home cultures to hear folks talk about issues from a biblical perspective that is more literally interpreted and to call members back to the foundations of the faith.

Members of Hearth and Home cultures appreciate the unchangeable nature of the message they proclaim and live. The clarity provided by their faith is readily translated into guidelines for living and transferable from one situation to another. The line between right and wrong is usually bright and readily articulated. They are often deeply engaged in the study of Scripture through individual devotions, small group Bible studies, and educational classes that tend to engage members directly in the biblical text. Where a clear biblical mandate is perceived, members of Hearth and Home cultures provide services to those in need, often with remarkable tenacity and perseverance.

Quadrant: Progressive-Adaptable Cultural Designation: Magi Primal Element: Wind Popular Image: Tour Bus Context/Setting: University, Research **AT ITS BEST** Rational Advocate Intellectual Powerful Efficient Deep knowledge Yoda **AT ITS WORST** Aloof Impersonal Unapproachable Theoretical Spock on steriods	Quadrant: Conservative-Adaptable Cultural Designation: Performance Primal Element: Fire Popular Image: Revivalist/Traveling Salvation Show Context/Setting: Entertainment/Internet **AT ITS BEST** Fun loving, lively Spontaneous Experiential Conversion/New life Relevant Han Solo **AT ITS WORST** Irresponsible Flaky Unpredictable Not serious Shallow R2D2 (just kidding)
Quadrant: Progressive-Settled Cultural Designation: Paraclete Primal Element: Water Popular Image: Hostel/Hospital Context/Setting: Boundary Community **AT ITS BEST** Warm Compassionate Healing Mentoring Accepting Mother Teresa **AT ITS WORST** Overly emotional Overwhelmed Naive Sentimental Don Quixote	Quadrant: Conservative-Settled Cultural Designation: Hearth and Home Primal Element: Earth Popular Image: Lincoln Logs Context/Setting: Traditional Community **AT ITS BEST** Stable Secure Dependable Clear Guardian Prodigal father **AT ITS WORST** Rigid Controlling System bound Empty fort Elder brother

Figure 9.2. Four Operating Systems

People in Hearth and Home cultures tend to understand that the call to faith is the call to come home in many different senses of the word. It is a call to return to a biblical faith or a faith best articulated at a point in the past. In more liturgical traditions, it may be a call to return to a previous style of worship, prayer book, or hymn book. Since Hearth and Home cultures often see themselves as a family, straying members are called to come back to the family where they will be welcomed with open arms and ready forgiveness.

Efforts to remove inactive adult children from the church roll are often seen as abandonment. Even an annual visit to the church at Christmas "counts." In more evangelical churches, issues are more focused on personal faith and conversion. Still, members are expected to become engaged with the "family," whether that takes the form of a small group or active participation in the single cell of a family-sized congregation.

Biblical themes that resonate with Hearth and Home cultures include those of home, homeland, families and children, and the cycle of birth, confirmation, conversion, marriage, family, and a faithful death. Hearth and Home cultures often value the regulation of behavior articulated in clear proscriptions such as the Ten Commandments. In addition, Hearth and Home cultures may have other sourcebooks that are important, such as ecclesiastical regulations, confessional documents, or worship standards.

Shadow

Because Hearth and Home cultures understand themselves as guardians of traditional understandings and practices, the positions they take may leave them open to the charge that they are simply resistant to change. Their tendency to focus on the concrete side of matters may lead to inordinate attachments to facilities and furnishings. If they lose their missional focus, they may retreat into a fortress mentality and find themselves becoming a diminishing, aging congregation.

If Hearth and Home cultures do not adequately explore the intellectual side of their faith, including the relationship of their tradition to contemporary issues, they may find that they are increasingly detached from the world they live in. In addition, the drive for spiritual and moral clarity on core issues may manifest itself in a lack of tolerance with one another, making them vulnerable to demoralizing conflicts. Unless some amount of change can be embraced, returning sons and daughters will not encounter the loving father but a house full of elder brothers . . . or a house with no one in it at all.

Progressive-Settled Operating Systems: Paraclete

We refer to churches in the progressive-settled quadrant as Paraclete systems. Paraclete churches are ultimately concerned with the development of communities that are intellectually open and reflective but pay attention to structure and ritual. At their best, this type of church operating system embraces those with different theological and spiritual perspectives and encompasses structures and practices that provide the external stability necessary for those seeking to develop and grow. A warm and hospitable community can make the church a potential haven for those in need of healing or recovery. It is common in Paraclete cultures to hear folks talk about hospitality, inclusiveness, and spiritual practice. While many members are clearly grounded in their own theological perspectives, Paraclete cultures tend to be less demanding of a particular understanding of the faith but more clear about the benefits of a particular liturgical tradition.

People in Paraclete cultures are comfortable with the unique spiritual path that each individual must follow, but they also believe that they have discovered important patterns of spiritual practice. They may focus on methods for identifying strengths, temperaments, preferences, or ability patterns of those in their community. In addition, they may be articulate about stages of spiritual and emotional development.

Paraclete cultures are uniquely equipped to focus on ministries of healing. Their openness can make them comfortable dealing with various expressions of human brokenness and the emotional and spiritual consequences of life's misfortunes. In a compassionate response to suffering, Paraclete cultures may develop counseling centers, spiritual direction, homeless shelters, food pantries, support groups, and recovery services. What is distinctive about Paraclete cultures is that members are often engaged in the frontline work of these ministries and not simply the sponsors of work that others do.

The biblical images that resonate with Paraclete cultures are those of the Spirit, the parables of Jesus, the ministry of Jesus himself, the wilderness hospitality to strangers found in the exodus, and the Genesis garden as a primal pattern of rhythm, harmony, balance, and goodness at the heart of creation.

Paraclete cultures value openness to others who think differently about their faith. Their focus on the unique, individual journey may leave them open to the charge that they are wishy-washy regarding values that are core to the larger church. If they choose the healing path, their care for others will often draw them into a more personal and private sphere with those they are helping, and others may misinterpret this as emotionally intrusive. Their tendency to focus on the positive potential in situations and people may make it difficult for them to deal with the harshness of some cultural and political realities. If these churches lose their missional focus, they may retreat into a cycle of well-intentioned activity where freedom of thought or individual pain becomes an excuse for mediocrity.

Shadow

If Paraclete cultures do not find a way to balance their openness with reasonable expectations of others, they may end up attracting more needs than the resources required to address those needs. Their admirable tendency to accept people where they are may not offer an adequate level of accountability that is also essential to wholeness. Paraclete cultures can get trapped in the onion syndrome, always another layer and lots of tears.

By developing a performance dimension to their lives, that is, the capacity to do something very well, Paraclete cultures add an appropriate level of expectation that can generate both strength and resources. This might be achieved through excellence in a number of areas, including liturgical arts, outstanding preaching, or architecture. Alternatively, it might mean emphasizing the power of the gospel to transform and not simply to comfort.

Progressive-Adaptable Operating Systems: Magi

We refer to churches in the progressive-adaptable quadrant as Magi systems. Magi churches are ultimately concerned with the rational integrity of their faith, the just application of faith to life, and the journey of understanding and discovery. Adherence to these values shapes the community, which, at its best, exhibits deep knowledge, open discourse, and intellectual curiosity. A penetrating analytic culture makes the church a powerful ally for those in need of advocacy and a formidable foe to those with a different perspective on an issue. It is common in Magi cultures to hear folks talk about issues from a systems perspective and the need to develop safeguards for those with minority status or who lack the power to protect themselves.

People in Magi cultures are not averse to the wandering aspect of the faith. Indeed, they often understand faith as the foundation for wandering. This wandering can take many forms. For some, it can take the form of literal journeys, with a significant percentage of members engaged in travel or pilgrimage, with international lecturers brought onsite, or with leaders engaged in international exchanges. For others, the wandering happens in one place and takes the form of intellectual development or liturgical exploration. It is for this reason that Magi cultures are often, though not always, located near university campuses, research facilities, or other academic populations.

The biblical images that resonate with Magi cultures include the story of the magi themselves, the children of Israel in the wilderness, the prophets who spoke to the people of God amid the constellation of exiles and returns, the women who traveled about in support of the ministry of Jesus, and the ministry of Jesus traveling around Judea and healing all those oppressed by evil.

Magi cultures value knowledge and understanding. For this reason, they can be perceived as aloof and unapproachable. Because their care for others is often expressed in terms of fairness or justice, others may misinterpret them as personally cold or uncaring. Their intellectual explorations may leave them open to the charge that they lack commitment to the core values that are important to others. Their tendency to focus on the conceptual side may make it more difficult for them to deal with facility and maintenance issues. If they lose their missional focus, they may retreat into esoteric debates and end up being defined by what they think rather than what they *personally* do.

Shadow

If Magi cultures do not adequately develop the Hearth and Home dimension to their community life, they may find relationships difficult to develop and sustain. They also may overestimate the power of reason to manage the nonrational elements of life, which may result in emotions that erupt unexpectedly and without a path for resolution. They may be so focused on larger issues that they underestimate their need for training to develop boundaries, interpersonal skills, conflict resolution, and trust.

Since their dominant reflexes prioritize rational understanding, they may not give proper weight to the role of emotion in persuading and enlisting support. Failing to realize that it is emotion that leads to action, they may become frustrated that their decisions do not bring about change. In their quest to be flexible, they also may not give enough voice to the values of commitment and clarity.

By developing the more relational, emotional, and structural aspects of their common life, Magi cultures can add the stability that will help provide sustainability over the longer term. This can also provide the cohesion that will help the community build an identity that is not focused on a particular issue.

Conservative-Adaptable Operating Systems: Performance

We refer to churches in the conservative-adaptable quadrant as Performance systems. Performance churches are ultimately concerned with an experiential faith presented in a way that people find accessible and compelling. At their best, these cultures serve as bridges between traditional understandings of Christian beliefs and contemporary life experiences. By fusing the Christian message with a variety of innovative messaging techniques, the distance between past and present is spanned in a way that increases the plausibility of the message for the target audience. Performance cultures are often able to create powerful experiences for participants that open people to alternative ways of looking at life. By helping people reframe their daily experiences as spiritual encounters and opportunities for growth, these churches lay the groundwork for compelling calls to conversion and renewal.

Performance cultures are concerned with what works now and discovering ways to increase the impact of their message rather than changing the basic message. Venue, furnishings, music, symbols, media are all means to an end and could be changed at any time if a better method is discovered for winning people to faith or strengthening the faith of the already won. It is common in performance cultures to hear members talk about experiences; testimonies; being moved, inspired, lifted up, spoken to, touched, or convicted. Worship services, witness talks, and group experiences are specially designed for an experiential impact that can lead to conversion and transformation.

Performance cultures often rely heavily on the performing arts. By presenting an ancient message using the best of contemporary media, Internet technology, or other innovative messaging approaches, performance cultures create experiences in which the emphasis is widened from simply understanding the gospel to feeling the power of it.

The biblical themes most resonant with Performance cultures are those that can be powerfully portrayed and experienced. Their preachers are often masters at retelling Bible stories of individual encounters with God in a way that pulls listeners into their own encounter. While the confrontation may be more indirect than that of a revivalist tent meeting, the result is the same: a crisis is created and a choice must be made. Performance cultures also resonate with the experiential quality of the psalms and may build much of their worship experience around simple verses set to music.

Performance culture efforts to make an eternal message fresh and accessible may leave them open to the charge that they fail to recognize the importance of a shared tradition. In addition, they may underestimate the creativity and resources required to be effective in their approach. The gap between the performance ideal in the mind and the actual lived reality may lead to a new tradition of mediocrity that fails its purpose. If Performance cultures lose their missional focus, they may find themselves chasing a religious high where lives are rarely changed and where the change that occurs does not have adequate roots to be sustainable.

Shadow

If Performance cultures do not adequately develop the deeper dimensions of their community life, they run the risks of shallowness and pretense. In their tendency to focus on conversion and transformation, they may not appreciate the often slow and painful process required for spiritual development and recovery from trauma. Their inability to acknowledge the abiding shadows within the human personality can lead to personal behaviors that are inconsistent with their public persona. By incorporating service to others, spiritual direction, and spiritual disciplines that have proved valuable to Christians across the centuries, Performance cultures can ground the gifts and creativity that give them such an impact upon the people around them.

Dead Zones

As I have noted, some strategies work in some churches and not in others. And there are some church operating systems *where nothing works*. These are dead zones. Most of us who own cell phones know about dead zones: an area where our calls are dropped because we do not have service. Sometimes we find to our dismay that those around us who use a different provider are getting their calls through just fine.

Over the years as I have worked with leaders in hundreds of congregations, we have been able to locate those dead zones on a map of the four types of operating systems in churches. The zones where nothing works are in the deep settled areas of the progressive and conservative quadrants. When churches self-disclose that they are located in those zones, we inevitably discover that they have heartbreakingly low levels of satisfaction and energy. Generally, less than a third of the members are clearly satisfied and a majority of members indicate that they are simply going through the motions of church activity. Ironically, these churches are the most insistent that priority be given to reaching new members. They are never able to succeed at this for two reasons. First, the operating system will not allow the changes that are required to reach new people. When attempts at change are made, conflict is generated that drives satisfaction and energy to even more desperate levels. Second, it does not take long for the new people who do join to realize that the system creates unhappy, de-energized people. Only people who have normalized these kinds of environments tend to stay in them.

The dead zone is only slightly different between conservative and progressive churches. Conservative churches tend to value clarity over tolerance, which makes differences more difficult to resolve. In addition to the low satisfaction and energy found in very settled progressive churches, they often have to deal with higher levels of conflict to boot. Thus the designation of Hospice to deeply settled conservative churches and ICU to deeply settled progressive churches. (See figure 9.3.) In contrast, adaptable churches do not have dead zones. This does not mean that all adaptable churches are flourishing. Due to a variety of factors other than flexibility, some adaptable churches are flourishing and some are not. That is the significance of a dead zone. A dead zone is a location on the map where a church cannot thrive, xor in some cases survive, no matter what else it does or how well it does it.

Progressive adaptable	Conservative adaptable
Progressive settled **ICU**	Conservative settled **HOSPICE**

Figure 9.3. Dead Zones in Settled Churches

On the face of it, this piece of organizational intelligence may seem discouraging for churches to come to terms with. Yet, is it any different from the personal insight that many of us have had to accept? How many of us are unconsciously sabotaging our best efforts to grow as individuals? We would like to flourish, but we are afraid of the jealousy of others, and so we find ways to turn down the volume of our giftedness. We would like to be joyful, but the guilt of our imperfections drives us to repeatedly stick a pin in the balloon of our happiness. The recognition of the contradictions within ourselves are liberating if we are willing to accept responsibility for the way we personally undermine our own well-being.

People often express surprise that the churches that are most unhappy tend to be those that are most insistent that nothing change. Is this really so strange? Is not the scriptural record an account of the greatest contradiction: that God created the universe in love yet humans consistently try to sever the cord to that creative source? Is not Jesus the one who gives us the truth that sets us free? And is it not the case that the liberating truth is often that we are sabotaging the very life we seek?

Contrary to the perceptions of many, organizational intelligence does not claim to provide all the answers. In many cases it clarifies the contradictions the Spirit is inviting us to face. An evidence-based discernment process is *a discernment process*—not the answer sheet to a test. Nor is it a recipe for success. The point is this: organizational intelligence does not guarantee success, but its absence almost certainly guarantees failure.

In the next chapter we will explore other important aspects of a church that organizational intelligence discloses, including the patterns of its shared life.

Discussion Questions

1. This chapter explores the idea that every church has an operating system, that is, an underlying organizational culture that may be invisible to members because they live in it. However, this system is so powerful that it determines what programs will run in the church and which ones will not. Besides the typical list of ideals that get named (love, Jesus, peace), what does your church *really* value, which forms the underlying operating system?

2. Organizational intelligence can help uncover the operating system of a church. Of the four operating systems named, Magi, Paraclete, Performance, and Hearth and Home, which do you believe best describes the operating system of your church? What are some of the strengths of that system? Have you ever seen the shadow side of your operating system hurt the church's ministries?

3. About 25 percent of the churches in the United States are in the Dead Zone (ICU or Hospice), which means that their operating systems are killing them.[2] Do you think it is important for a church to know that about themselves? How would you go about giving them that news?

CHAPTER 10

Taking an X-Ray of Your Church

Interesting phenomena occur when two or more rhythmic patterns are combined, and these phenomena illustrate very aptly the enrichment of information that occurs when one description is combined with another.

—Gregory Bateson, English anthropologist, 1904–1980

W hen the leadership of a church engages in an evidenced-based discernment process and has access not only to count data but also to witness data—the perspectives, experiences, and aspirations of the members they lead and serve—they begin to get a snapshot of the congregation. As important as that snapshot is, more is possible. What is possible is an X-ray, which helps people see underlying patterns. Organizational intelligence is like an X-ray; it makes patterns visible. Pattern awareness can help leaders be more successful in their discernment process much as X-rays can help doctors be more effective in healing.

The Importance of Patterns

We call something a pattern when we notice that two or more things tend to occur together. Every life has its patterns. Some patterns are obvious and appear immediately. Some must be discovered over time. I have been married to my wife, Shawn, for about four years. I discovered early in our relationship that for her, getting up in the morning was characterized by movement from one place to another in short, shuffling steps, squinting eyes, and a sluggish mental state in which making even small decisions seemed a daunting task.

Then she would have her morning coffee. Over the course of about twenty minutes, a new person slowly emerged, one who was agile, bright, and decisive. It did not take me too long to discover that "cup of coffee" consistently appeared with "agile, bright, and decisive." Being aware of this pattern has guided my morning behavior and has helped me be more successful in our relationship. I have also learned to make coffee.

Every church has patterns to its life. Some of these patterns are visible: weekly worship, monthly board meetings, annual celebrations like Christmas and Easter. Other important patterns are less visible or even invisible.

The Pattern of Spiritual Practice and Giving

A practical example may help illustrate how organizational intelligence helps to make patterns visible. We can see this in members' spiritual practices and their giving. In addition to the corporate spiritual life that members share in worship, there is individual spiritual practice as well. When members bear witness to this individual aspect, they speak of a variety of spiritual experiences that affect how they view life. They may speak of the ways in which they experience God's presence in their lives. Others may bear witness to extending the impact of their faith into the whole of their lives—family life, work life, and friendships.

Members also support the ministries of the church by sharing their resources. This has been traditionally capsulized as time, talent, and treasure. With regard to treasure, Christian theology has generally affirmed the principle of proportionate giving. Using the account of the widow's mite from the New Testament as the paradigm, it is not how much you give that is the question; it is how much you give compared to what you possess. For churches, this means that the key metric for the generosity of the congregation is the average percentage of household income given to the church. Note that this information is witness data. It cannot be known unless members disclose how much money they make.

A contrast with other organizations may be instructive. Over the years, I have worked with a number of libraries that need help gauging the level of support in their communities for a local ballot issue that would increase taxes in order to sustain or expand library services. Armed with that intelligence, we are able to help libraries shape their appeal based upon the needs in the community. Our track record is pretty good. We can predict with 90 percent accuracy the outcome of those elections. Most church leaders have nothing comparable to this level of intelligence regarding member perspectives on giving.

In my work with congregations, I have noticed this pattern: when the members of a church as a group bear witness to a more vibrant individual spiritual practice, we also observe that they give a larger percentage of household income to the church. We now have pattern awareness of the relationship between individual spiritual practice and financial giving to the church.

Implicit Patterns

Just as every leaf on a tree shares in a particular pattern, every member of a church participates in a set of patterned behaviors. When we look at the pattern of spiritual practice and giving, we learn some things about patterns in general.

- Patterns are often not discovered from count data alone. Members must bear witness to both their individual spiritual experience and their household income for it to be observable to those around them. We can't "see" faith.
- Patterns are often difficult to identify through discussions at town meetings, focus groups, or planning retreats. Even if members were comfortable sharing all the pertinent information in a meeting, it would not be a reliable indicator for the entire congregation.
- Patterns are often not intuitively obvious. For many leaders, increasing giving is a matter of a better stewardship campaign in November. (An evidence-based discernment process discloses a number of patterns that are not intuitively obvious, which makes it even more important that we discover them.)
- Patterns often have important long-term implications. In the case of spiritual practices and giving, the pattern suggests that a strategic approach to expanding the ministries of the church is best achieved by deepening the spiritual practice and experience of individual members.

These are called *implicit patterns*. Implicit patterns vary from church to church. How well a leadership team discovers and deals with these patterns is often the difference between success and failure. We now turn our attention to three of the most important implicit patterns.

The Pattern of Clergy-Focused Churches

When we examine the organizational intelligence generated from churches, one pattern we discover is that members' evaluations of the church's ministry overall is strongly determined by how they evaluate some aspect of the work of the pastor. We refer to churches that exhibit this pattern as clergy-focused churches. What is surprising about this clergy-focused pattern is not that it exists but how pervasive it often is. We will explore the characteristics of a clergy-focused church by examining the organizational intelligence from St. Bridget's Church summarized in figure 10.1.

Name of Church:	*St. Bridget's Church*
Vitality Status:	*Chaos*
Member focus:	*Clergy-focused*
Critical success factors:	*How well the pastor's plan insures pastoral care*
Level of criticality:	*Very high*
Priority Focus:	*Magi*

Figure 10.1. St. Bridget's Church Organizational Intelligence Profile.
For a definition of terms, please see the glossary in appendix A.

How members evaluate the work of the pastor is the lens through which members view the entire church. Figures 10.2 and 10.3 help make this clear. Here, additional organizational intelligence from a church (its name has been changed) is displayed as a dashboard with gauges. The first gauge displays how members feel about the hospitality level of the church, another, how members feel about the educational ministry of the church, another, how members feel about the readiness of members to engage in ministry, and another, how members feel about the worship and music in the church. In every case, a higher reading on the gauge, with the needle farther to the right, indicates a higher evaluation.

Notice that worship and music is directly affected by the work of the pastor. However, hospitality, education, and readiness for ministry arguably have more to do with the people in the church or the impact of other leaders. Both dashboards are from the same church. The dashboard in figure 10.2 displays the information from members who agree that the pastor does a good job bringing out the best in people. The dashboard in figure 10.3 displays the information from members who do not feel the pastor does a good job bringing out the best in people.

What is striking in this church is that members are evaluating nearly everything in the church through the lens of how they feel about the pastor.

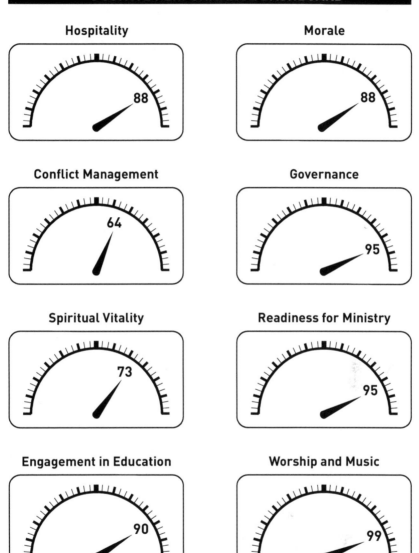

POSITIVE PERFORMANCE DASHBOARD

Hospitality
88

Morale
88

Conflict Management
64

Governance
95

Spiritual Vitality
73

Readiness for Ministry
95

Engagement in Education
90

Worship and Music
99

Figure 10.2. How Members Who Feel Positive about the Pastor See the Church

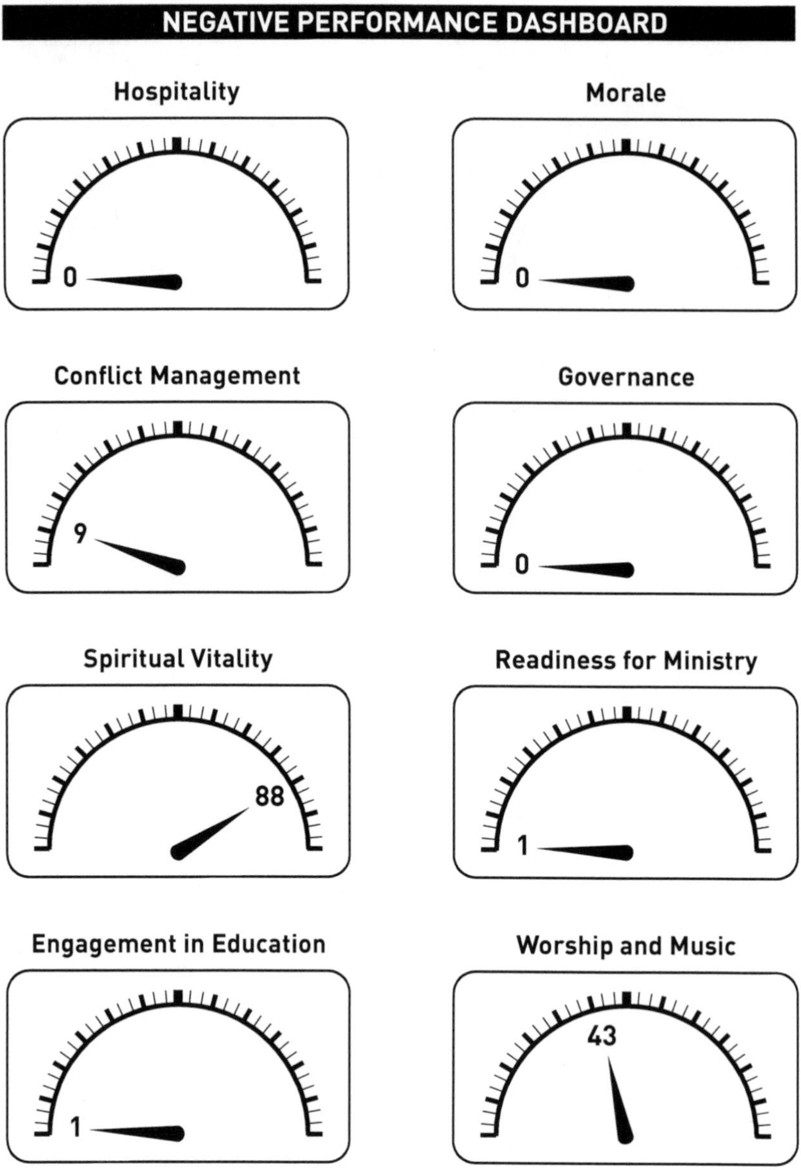

Figure 10.3. How Members Who Feel Negative about the Pastor See the Church

For people who feel more positive about the work of the pastor, the church has one of the best educational ministries in the country. For people who feel more negative about the work of the pastor, the church has one of the worst educational ministries in the country. For people who feel more positive about the work of the pastor, the church is one of the most hospitable churches in the country. For those who feel more negative about the work of the pastor, the church is one of the least hospitable churches in the country.

What we are observing in this clergy-focused church is an implicit pattern. *It cannot be discovered by count data alone.* Leaders would not be able to look at data on membership, worship attendance, or giving and discover this pattern. They might have hunches that trends in the church, up or down, were related to how people felt about the pastor, but they would only be hunches. They could be wrong. Even if they were right, their hunches would not give them enough confidence to act.

It would be difficult to identify through traditional meetings. The traditional way that leaders often go about gathering information is through focus groups or listening sessions. The problem is that these groups usually involve too few people to provide reliable information on the entire organization. The number of folks willing to attend a focus group is generally a small fraction, often less than a quarter of the people actually involved in the organization. After talking with twenty people from an organization with one hundred members, about one in five of the conclusions about the entire organization is likely to be wrong. Also, the information collected from focus groups is skewed toward the opinions of those who are more outspoken and extraverted. In addition, cultivating candid conversations in focus groups requires a high degree of trust that may not exist in the organization.

The pattern is not intuitively obvious. You might object here: "Of course it is the case that members determine how they feel about the church based upon how they feel about the pastor. That is true in every church!" First, as we shall see, it is not true in every church. Second, it would be surprising to most people to realize that how people feel about the pastor is affecting how they feel about ministries in the church that have nothing to do with the pastor.

Third, churches may have developed so much language about lay ministry that it makes it difficult for them to face the degree to which members do not recognize those lay ministries as having merit in and of themselves. In fact, these churches are often crazy-making for pastors who simultaneously feel the burden of the church on their shoulders while being told that they should step aside and let the laypeople run things.

The pattern has important long-term implications. When a church is clergy-focused, all attempts to increase a sense of well-being among the membership by expanding or improving ministries are doomed to fail. A church could excel in education and spiritual formation, mount the most extensive mission program in the country, and have a superb outreach to new people in the community. While each of these would be worthwhile from the standpoint of the kingdom of God, they are unlikely to improve how people are feeling in a clergy-focused church where a significant number of people are unhappy with the pastor. As a result, they are not sustainable. In a clergy-focused church, the pastor must be a person who is comfortable on center stage, is committed to spending his or her reputational capital to develop and support other ministries, and has an ego that is appropriately bounded. Clearly this pattern affects strategy, tactics, pastoral fit, and leadership tasks, all major items on the discernment checklist.

In a clergy-focused church where members feel positive about the pastor, almost anything will work, from the standpoint of members feeling positive and energized by the church. In a clergy-focused church where members are less positive about the pastor, almost nothing will work. If the strategic plan in a clergy-focused church with a low evaluation of the pastor does not address how to change the way members perceive the pastor, it will be difficult to change much else.

The Pattern of Power-Focused Churches

Not every church is clergy-focused. Some churches are power-focused.

In power-focused churches, we discover that members who feel more positive about the church overall are the same members who feel more positive about the people in power, the degree to which they believe leaders represent them, and whether leaders are taking their views into account, and vice versa. I have chosen not to lengthen the book by adding dashboards, but if I had, you would see that they are nearly identical to those in figures 10.2 and 10.3, with one crucial difference: the critical factor is not the pastor but how people perceive the power within the church. As in clergy-focused churches, the members' perspective on the people in power and how they are making decisions washes out any meaningful consideration of the other ministries of the church. While it is possible to have a clergy-focused church that is vital and growing, churches that are powercentric are almost always conflicted. Again, all attempts to increase a sense of well-being among the membership by expanding or improving ministries will have limited success if a significant number of people are not feeling positive about their relationship to the leadership. This pattern also affects strategy, tactics, pastoral fit, and leadership tasks.

The Pattern of Ministry-Focused Churches

The final implicit pattern I want to mention is the ministry-focused church. In this church, how people are feeling about the church overall is affected by how they feel about the ministries of the church (or how people are being supported in those ministries). A lot fits into this basket. It can include education, spiritual formation, helping members identify gifts, preparing people for ministry, hospitality, diversity, worship, music, and more. Many people would see this pattern as the ideal. Arguably, it is the vision of ministry that most clergy aspire to and are trained for.

In fact, each implicit pattern has its strengths and weaknesses. Ministry-focused churches are potentially less volatile, but they may also be slower to turn than clergy-focused churches. Clergy-focused churches usually have higher levels of anxiety, even if things are going well. However, a strong pastor in a clergy-focused church can get a lot accomplished in a relatively short period of time. Power-focused churches are subject to high levels of conflict that sometimes can only be remedied by drastic measures. Nonetheless, when these systems find a way to bring people into consensus, sometimes by flattening the organizational structure, sometimes through a pastor with the savvy to form an amalgam from conflicting interests, they also can marshal a significant amount of energy for good purposes.

Pastors Have Patterns Too

Just as churches exhibit different patterns in the way they function, pastors exhibit patterns as well. Some are internally wired to function by creating and supporting a number of high-impact, lay-driven ministries. Some are internally wired to take center stage and use their reputational capital to generate resources for ministries that are important to them. Still others are internally wired to build coalitions across diverse groups in order to accomplish common goals. Just as there are ministry-focused, clergy-focused, and power-focused churches, there are ministry-focused, clergy-focused, and power-focused pastors.

A word to pastors: if you are a ministry-focused pastor in a clergy-focused church, your first impulse (and often your training) is going to involve creating an array of ministries aligned to a particular vision for the future. However, you may be frustrated to discover that many people just don't care. They care about your ability to create a positive connection with them. The connection can be generated pastorally, through winning your allegiance to their cause or through pride of affiliation with you. You will not be able to easily sidestep this issue. You will need to find a way to create energy through your connections and leverage that energy for the ministries you believe are important. Or you may decide to try to change the pattern. Or you may decide to seek a call that is a better fit.

Clergy-focused pastors in ministry-focused churches will also be challenged. Your first impulse will be to take center stage in order to move the church rapidly toward objectives you believe are important. However, you may become frustrated with how slowly things move in a ministry-focused system. You may have to adapt to the reality that slow change is often more durable in the long run. Or try to change the pattern. Or seek a call that is a better fit.

Similar issues arise in the mismatch between clergy and churches in power-focused patterns. To do well in power-focused systems, clergy will need conflict management skills combined with the ability to create organizational structures and processes where decision making is relatively open and power is shared. Clearly, pastoral fit is a major issue. One promise of evidence-based discernment is a better fit between pastors and the churches that call them.

Shifting Patterns

Can implicit patterns be changed? This question is part of a larger discussion that goes well beyond the scope of this book. Ever so briefly, let's go back to my wife and her morning coffee. One option would be for me to adapt to her pattern, make sure she has coffee, and delay any demanding conversation until after it kicks in. The other option would be for me to wean her off coffee and find an alternative way to jumpstart her morning. Which road would you take?

Yes, implicit patterns can be changed, but the change will generally require

- a consensus from a critical mass that the change is necessary,
- strong leadership from the top,
- a willingness to endure some losses, and
- three to five years of consistent, hard work.

My question for leaders is this: Do you really want to go to battle without a clear understanding of what you are dealing with? Getting clarity on this question is part of the promise of evidence-based discernment.

Peer Awareness

The leadership team of St. Anywhere Church is engaged in an evidence-based discernment process that has collected some organizational intelligence from the church. From the witness of their members, they have discovered that 20 percent of the congregation indicates that they are simply going through the motions of church activity. Let's tune in on the conversation:

DON: This is a result that gives me great concern. Think of it! One out of five of our members sitting in those pews every Sunday thinks we are simply marking time!

MARY: I have to agree with Don. I have been saying for some time that we have lost a sense of purpose in this church. Something needs to change.

JOE: Hold on a minute. I think this is just the way it is in churches. Every church has a few people that aren't really on board.

ANN: I understand that, Joe. But 20 percent of them? That's a lot of people. I'll bet they don't have this problem in the Baptist church down the street.

JOE: I still say it's nothing to worry about. What I am worried about is that 25 percent of our members are saying they are disturbed by the level of conflict in the church.

DON: Oh, that doesn't bother me. I think that's just the way it is in churches.

MARY: There have to be some other churches in our denomination that have figured out how to deal with some of these issues. Let's do some research.

ANN: I'm not sure that is a good use of our time. In our denomination, all the churches are in decline. We're all pretty much in the same boat.

You can hear these kinds of conversations going on in the boardrooms of churches across the United States. In the absence of an external reference point, leaders can make big mistakes. They may overreact to issues that are not a large problem and they may underreact to other issues that can send the church into a downward spiral from which it may be difficult to recover. Time and time again, I have seen leaders argue for the status quo, because they are relying only on their own internal perceptions without an external reference point.

The Importance of an External Reference Point

Having an external reference point is called peer awareness. Peer awareness is something we possess and make use of all the time. If you had never seen a two-year-old in your entire life and you saw one for the very first time, you would be likely to say to yourself, "There is something seriously wrong with this little person!" We don't do that because we have peer awareness, that is, we are aware of what two-year-olds are like. When we see a two-year-old, we don't compare him with adults that we know (well, most adults that we know). We compare him to a group of his peers. Having some two-year-old peer awareness, we can say when a particular two-year-old is "just being a two-year-old" or when he is exceptional in one way or another (depending on if it is mine or yours).

If the leaders of St. Anywhere Church had peer awareness, they would be able to say that a church where only 20 percent of the members indicate they are going through the motions is one of the most energized churches in the United States. They would also be able to say that having 25 percent of the members disturbed by the level of conflict in the church is not "how it is in churches" and probably indicates a significant problem that needs to be addressed. And, in fact, not every church in any denomination is in decline; there are some transformational exceptions that are noteworthy. Don, Mary, Joe, and Ann are each right about some things and wrong about other things, largely because they do not have an external reference point. The lack of peer awareness can be extremely disorienting. Peer awareness restores a sense of what is up and what is down.

Answering an Objection

Sometimes people object to peer awareness by saying something like this: "We're not in competition with other churches. Why should we care about how we stack up against other churches?" The answer depends upon the mission of the particular church. If a church is internally focused and has no interest in reaching hurting people outside its doors, peer awareness is much less important. However, if it wants to reach people, all that changes. When a person in need of God's grace and healing walks into your church for the first time, is it important that, *by the witness of your own members,* the person would find a warmer welcome in 90 percent of the other churches in your community? When a person going through a marriage breakup walks into your church for the first time, is it important that, *by the witness of your own members,* he or she would find a less conflicted environment in 80 percent of the other churches in your community?

In a discernment process, peer awareness can provide some guidance regarding what is typical . . . and what is not. In some cases, we may believe that God wants us to shoot for something more than what is typical, to set a new standard for what it means to be a Christian church. In other cases, we may discern that we are called to let it be. I have a counselor who has said to me, "Russ, sometimes you just have to say, 'It's good enough!'"

We have offered the view that evidence-based discernment is an integration of love, knowledge, and insight to discern what is best for a church. We have suggested that the organizational intelligence required for such a process includes count data and witness data encompassing the perspectives, the experiences, and the aspirations of the people we are called to lead and serve. A deep look at the organizational intelligence discloses implicit patterns that serve as a kind of X-ray of a particular expression of the body of Christ. Finally, peer awareness is an aspect of organizational intelligence that serves as a corrective to the disorientation that can occur when leaders have no external reference point to establish where they are.

I have already alluded to some of the promises of an evidence-based discernment process. I will close this chapter by mentioning a few others and bringing them together in a final list.

- Evidence-based discernment can help leaders know what strategies and tactics are more likely to be fruitful in a particular congregation and which are not.
- Evidence-based discernment can guide pastors and churches in the calling process toward a better fit.
- Evidence-based discernment can help leaders do a better job managing pastoral transitions (more on this to come in later chapters).
- Evidence-based discernment can reduce conflict in leadership teams regarding the current state of the church.
- Evidence-based discernment can help resolve conflict in congregations by letting members know they have been heard.
- Evidence-based discernment can free leaders to invest their energy in the more creative aspects of the discernment process, such as prayer, meditation, reading, and conversations with other leaders.
- Evidence-based discernment can provide better estimates regarding resources in the church and ways to mobilize them.
- Evidence-based discernment can help surface for the kingdom the aspirations of members that are currently unexpressed and untapped.
- Evidence-based discernment can help spot problems in the early stages before irreversible damage occurs.

For those who serve local congregations as regional executives or consultants, evidence-based discernment can help shape their interactions and interventions with a leadership team. While we often say that every church is distinct and requires a customized approach, we generally don't have the organizational intelligence that enables us to provide anything other than generic, one-size-fits-all methodologies.

This marks the end of part 2, the structure of organizational intelligence. In the next section, we turn our attention to an application of OI that I have found to be of particular importance to church leaders, OI and succession planning. Every church is distinct, and those distinctives become especially important during a pastoral search process. That is the subject of the next chapter.

Discussion Questions

1. If you could wave a magic wand and turn your church into either a ministry-focused church, a power-focused church, or a clergy-focused church, which one would you choose? What makes your choice better than the other two? How would your church be different if your wish were granted?

2. Some churches are clergy-focused; members tend to see everything through the lens of how they feel about the pastor. What do you think it is like to be a member of a clergy-focused church? What do you think it is like to serve on a board in a clergy-focused church? What do you think it is like to be the pastor of a clergy-focused church?

3. Do you think it is important to know how your church compares to other churches? Let's say, for example, that someone were to come up to you and say, "I am sick of a few people doing all the work around here." Let's say that you had the organizational intelligence showing that in actuality your church shares the work better than 95 percent of the churches in the United States. Is it important to be able to say that?

PART 3

Organizational Intelligence and Succession Planning

CHAPTER 11

A Customized Approach to Church Leadership

Fear, conformity, immorality: these are heavy burdens. They drain us of creative energy. And when we are drained of creative energy, we do not create. We procreate, but we do not create.

—David McCallum, playing the character of Gwyllm Griffiths in "The Sixth Finger," an episode of *The Outer Limits*

L awrence LeShan is not a household name across the United States, even though many who are aware of his work consider him to be the father of the mind-body movement. In reflecting on my life's journey, if I had to pick one writer who has had the greatest practical impact on my life and work, it would be Lawrence LeShan.

LeShan is a classically trained psychologist. Early in his career he began working with terminally ill cancer patients. At first LeShan used the classic psychotherapeutic approach he was trained in, where the model was to uncover what was wrong with the patient and then determine what could be done about it. Was there something dark and hidden within the patient's psyche? Could it be brought to light and either cured or compensated for?

This traditional analytic approach can have very positive effects with many types of mental, emotional, and behavioral issues, but LeShan maintains that it did not prove helpful in mobilizing the immune system—something cancer patients must immediately accomplish if they are to survive. During the time he used this classical approach, almost none of his cancer patients survived their diagnosis longer that what had been predicted.

Frustrated and burned out, LeShan took a long sabbatical and retreated to Europe. There he struck upon a different approach. He began to wonder what would happen if he asked,

> What is right with this person? What are his or her special and unique ways of being, relating, creating, that are his own and natural ways to live? What is his special music to beat out in life, his unique song to sing so that when he is singing it he is glad to get up in the morning and glad to go to bed at night? What style of life would give him zest, enthusiasm, involvement?[1]

One of the questions that LeShan came up with was this:

> Let us suppose that your fairy godmother will come in that door in a few minutes. She will make you an offer. In six months your inner and outer life can be exactly what you would like it to be so that you would use yourself most completely and have the maximum enjoyment and zest possible. You can change your feelings and your circumstances. There are no limitation on age sex, education and so forth.[2]

LeShan returned to the States and began putting his new approach into practice. His patients found the question both exhilarating and terrifying. To his amazement he found that when people committed to finding the life that really *fit* them, approximately half of his cancer patients with poor prognoses went into long-term remission and many are still alive. In every case, people did not feel the same.

Organizational Intelligence and a Tailored Approach

How might LeShan's remarkable findings with individuals apply to congregations?

As I suggested in chapter 3, denominational churches and systems tend to be administratively robust. They excel at the development of policies and procedures designed to address the typical issues that congregations face. As a result, they are best at developing standardized approaches and focusing on compliance issues. Absent any reliable way of distinguishing the needs of one congregation from another, they have no choice but to employ one-size-fits-all approaches. Unfortunately, the congregations that have discovered effective approaches to ministry tend also to be the ones that have colored outside the lines. Highly standardized approaches not only penalize creativity and innovation but they also are unable to gauge the factors in a particular congregation that are impeding its ability to claim its better life. At an organizational scale, cancer develops when a church fails to discover and embrace its fundamental purpose. It begins to function in a mechanical fashion that is fully compliant in all its administrative functions but lacks spiritual zest. Sooner or later, its immune system is compromised and a variety of opportunistic diseases (conflict, dysfunctional behaviors, burnout, and so forth) begin to invade the body.

One promise of organizational intelligence is that it enables those who care about churches—pastors, denominational leaders, and consultants—to deal with congregations as distinct communities with their own signatures and requiring their own tailored approach. In a chapter found in *The Leader-Manager*, George Ainsworth-Land makes an important observation: "Now we see that all management theories are correct. Every past theory that has been discovered refers to a different period in an organization's and an individual's lifecycle."[3] If leaders, denominational resource people, and consultants are going to be effective in helping churches, they require much better tools that can help them understand where a church is.

Succession Processes

Nowhere is this more clearly illustrated than with churches in a succession process. There are a variety of approaches for helping churches in succession. Unfortunately, they are all true, but true for churches in different situations.

A classical approach to churches in a succession process would argue that churches in pastoral transition need an interim pastor who serves a period of twelve to twenty-four months between the departure of the former pastor and the arrival of the next pastor. That's true in some cases, but not in others. Some churches can do fine without an interim pastor.

Another accepted truism is that long-term pastorates are more certain to require the services of an interim pastor serving a correspondingly longer period of time before the arrival of the next pastor. However, that's true in some cases but not in all. Some churches love their long-term pastor but, frankly, are ready for a change. What's more, they can read a calendar. Retirement does not come as a shock.

Another commonly accepted understanding is that, absent the services of an interim pastor, the successor pastor will become an unintentional interim. A better way of saying this is that the failure to address transitional issues requires that they be addressed by the next pastor. Having an interim does not insure that this has been accomplished.

In another approach, succession processes in churches are addressed primarily as emotional passages rather than strategic, missional opportunities and the conversation is dominated by words like sadness, anger, remorse, fear, confusion, loss, grief, depression, and so forth. This is true again in some cases. But in many cases the church is more strategic in its orientation and more focused on how to sustain its ministries across the transition than on how to deal with its emotions.

Another view interprets all struggles in the church through the lens of a "good" or "bad" pastoral transition. One unwritten job description of a good pastor is to hold a dysfunctional element of the congregation in check. This element might be a tendency toward divisiveness, a chronic jealousy of folks in leadership, or a penchant to hearken for the good ole days, which, in many ways, were not so good. These tendencies can stymie a church unless the pastor plays an active role in preventing it from happening. My friend Linda Karlovec, a psychologist and consultant, calls this "tending the organizational cowlick." The cowlick never goes away. By the strength of his or her own leadership, wisdom, and political capital, the pastor keeps the dysfunction from metastasizing throughout the church. When an effective pastor steps back, these elements tend to emerge. If the leadership misreads this as, for example, the anger stage of loss and encourages its expression as part of the healing process, tremendous damage can result. When dysfunctional behaviors are normalized and excused as grief reactions, it often does not result in insight, it tends to incite.

I have found this difficult for many leaders to accept, given the therapeutic methodology that has held sway among interim ministers. Church business administrators are a different story. Speaking on the subject of church transitions at a national meeting of church business administrators in 2005, I saw a number of nodding heads when I spoke about long-term dysfunctional behaviors emerging during transitions. When I asked the group why they so easily "got that," someone said to me afterwards, "Because all the crazies come out, and we are left to deal with them." Organizational intelligence can help a leadership team know whether they are dealing with a natural grief reaction or a longer-term issue. It all depends upon the situation.

My experience is that a successful pastoral transition depends on where a church is. I sometimes get a message from a church leader that says something like this: "We tried a succession process using an interim pastor and it was terrible." On the other hand, I sometimes get a message from a church leader that says something like this: "We tried a succession process without using an interim pastor and it was terrible." One promise of organizational intelligence is that it can support an evidence-based discernment process in pastoral transitions that distinguishes what one church needs from what another church might need. This avoids a one-size-fits-all approach, on the one hand, while mitigating the tendencies of a congregation to minimize transitional issues on the other. How do churches generate that intelligence?

When I first began to work in the area of pastoral transition, I acted like a medieval scholar debating where a stone dropped from the crow's nest would strike the deck of a moving ship. I wondered how people would deal with a pastoral transition, but it took awhile before it occurred to me to actually ask them. In the witness data provided by members, a church can gather several pieces of organizational intelligence that are critical in shaping a succession process that fits its particular situation. That organizational intelligence includes a basic assessment of the perspectives, experiences, and aspirations of the members of the church, and also includes the following:

The anticipated change in member involvement during the pastoral transition.

- The availability of members to help with transitional tasks.
- The anticipated change in member giving during the pastoral transition.
- The number of members who will explore other churches during the pastoral transition.
- The level of comfort members have with the timing of the transition.
- The degree to which members believe the leadership represents them.
- The amount of change required in the church's direction.
- The amount of change required in the responsibilities of the next pastor compared to the former pastor.

In the next few pages, I will describe three components of a succession process and how organizational intelligence helps shape each one.

How Organizational Intelligence Shapes a Succession Plan

A succession plan comprises these components: a transition plan, a search plan, and a start-up plan.

The *transition plan* outlines how the leadership team, with or without an interim pastor, will manage the period of time from the resignation announcement of the pastor to the arrival of the next pastor. It addresses the following factors.

In any situation it is always important to capitalize upon opportunities. In the typical church roughly 20 percent of members (net)[4] indicate they will become more involved in the church. This represents an opportunity. But this is where the organizational intelligence for a *particular* congregation is vital. For a particular Anglican church in Canada, that number is zero! For a Presbyterian church in Pennsylvania it is 41 percent! One church has an opportunity to be realized that does not exist in the other. In a church where the current member engagement is low and the indicated increase in their involvement is high, a transition plan will tap that energy and generate a level of excitement and momentum that the next pastor can help carry forward. In a church where the current engagement of members is high and the indicated increase in their involvement is low, leaders will need to be careful about starting new initiatives during the transition. They will not want to have an exhausted church waiting for the new pastor to arrive.

Even more significant is the fact that in the typical church, about 30 percent of members (net) indicate that they will be more available to help with transition tasks. In some churches that number can be as high as 50 percent. In other words, in a church with 500 active members, as many as 250 of them indicate they want to help with the transition! Not everyone can serve on a search committee. A transition plan in this church will need to create meaningful ways for many people to become engaged. They might include prayer, event planning, communication, cosmetic improvements to facilities, assisting with worship, and calling on the sick. However, the same plan would totally overwhelm and defeat a church where only 10 percent of the members indicate their availability to help. It all depends upon the organizational intelligence.

Money is always an issue for churches in transition, partly due to search expenses but also due to the impact of uncertainty. However, we find that, on average, 15 percent of members (net) indicate that their giving level will be higher or much higher. This represents a significant opportunity in the typical church. In some churches as many as 25 percent of members indicate they will give more money during the transition. But in other churches members indicate that their overall giving will actually drop. A transition plan in a church where income is likely to increase by 25 percent is going to be quite different from the plan in a church where income is likely to drop by 10 percent. It all depends upon the organizational intelligence.

I do not want to belabor this point but I want to be clear: the organizational intelligence for churches in transition varies greatly from one church to another, and the plan for managing that transition should reflect those differences in a way that capitalizes on opportunities and manages risks.

Figure 11.1 illustrates this point by examining the organizational intelligence from two real churches. In one church (referred to as the low-opportunity, high-risk church), 22 percent of members indicate they will be more involved in the transition, but the same number (22 percent) indicate they will be less involved. In the second church (referred to as the high-opportunity, low-risk church), 41 percent indicate they will be more involved in the transition and only 1 percent indicate they will be less involved. These two churches must be managed quite differently in the succession process.

Opportunity and Risk Factors	Low-Opportunity, High-Risk Church	High-Opportunity, Low-Risk Church
Member involvement during the transition	22% more involved 22% less involved	41% more involved 1% less involved
Member availability to help with transition tasks	25% more available 30% less available	51% more available 7% less available
Member giving during transition	6% higher 11% lower	27% higher 3% lower
Members explore other churches during the transition	10% Clearly will 50% Clearly will not	0% Clearly will 84% Clearly will not
*Members comfortable with timing of pastoral transition	16% Clearly are 40% Clearly are not	56% Clearly are 4% Clearly are not
Leaders need to be more representative	53% Clearly agree 14% Clearly disagree	16% Clearly agree 47% Clearly disagree
Members want to continue in same direction	12% clearly agree 49% clearly disagree	64% Clearly agree 1% Clearly disagree
Members want same pastor responsibilities	13% Clearly agree 44% Clearly disagree	75% Clearly agree 3% Clearly disagree

Figure 11.1. Opportunity and Risk Factors for Churches in Succession

I have highlighted and asterisked a particular item in the figure, "Members comfortable with timing of pastoral transition." This is a bellwether data point in the organizational intelligence for a congregation in transition. When a significant percentage of the congregation indicates that they are not comfortable with the timing of the transition, it often signals that members are going to have a difficult time letting go of the former pastor. When combined with a high percentage of members who want the next pastor to have the same responsibilities, the insight provided by the organizational intelligence is clear: significant time and energy will need to be invested in helping people deal with the loss of the former pastor. In most cases, this will require the services of a trained and seasoned interim pastor.

So what is normal? How do we know when the percentages indicate a problem and when they are simply typical scores of churches in transition? We make that decision the same way we decide if our child is developing on schedule: we benchmark the church against other churches.

When Does the Organizational Intelligence Suggest an Interim Is Needed?

Figure 11.2 is a transition profile for a strong, mainline church with a long-tenured pastor who is retiring. The longer the bar, the higher the church's score compared to other churches. The shorter the bar, the lower the its score compared to other churches.

Notice in this particular profile the warning signs of a difficult transition. There is a very low level of comfort with the timing of the transition. (The bar is not missing. It is zero.) Notice also that members want the next pastor to do almost exactly what the former pastor did. Taken together these two indicators argue strongly for an interim pastor. In fact, the church chose not to use the services of an interim pastor but went straight to an installed pastor. Two years later the handwriting is on the wall. The new pastor is already looking for another call.

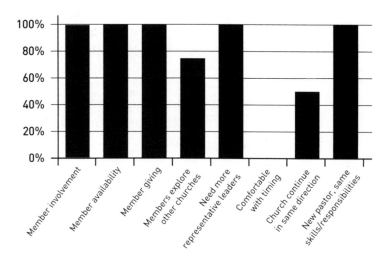

Figure 11.2. Warning Signs of a Difficult Transition

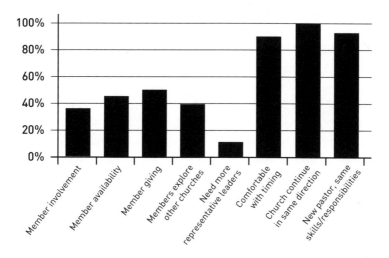

Figure 11.3. Signs of a Positive Transition

Contrast this transition profile with the one in figure 11.3, also from a mainline church with a long-tenured pastor who is retiring. This also is a strong church, and members want the next pastor to have roughly the same responsibilities as the previous one. The significant difference in the organizational intelligence is in the very high level of comfort members indicate regarding the timing of the transition. In this case I recommended that the church begin its search while the previous pastor remained on board, without the services of an interim pastor. The new pastor has been on board now for more than three years, and the church continues to flourish under his leadership. It all depends upon the organizational intelligence.

Organizational Intelligence and the Search Plan

The *search plan* specifies the critical requirements for a pastor who is a good fit for a church and the parameters of the search process. The importance of not only collecting but also paying attention to organizational intelligence is illustrated in the following experience.

First Presbyterian Church of Summerville was preparing to engage in a search process and decided to collect organizational intelligence from their congregation before proceeding. The assessment revealed that the congregation was high in satisfaction but low in energy. It also revealed a church that was clearly of a more progressive theological perspective. They then prepared the standard documents required by the denomination and began their search.

On their journey, they discovered a pastor in his fifties who had had a fruitful ministry at a church in another part of the state. What resonated with them was that he had an energy and excitement about his faith that was currently lacking in their church. They found him easy to connect with, warm, and exhibiting a heartfelt concern in his interactions. Finally, they liked the sermon they heard him preach as part of their search process.

What they did not do was refer to the organizational intelligence they had collected in order to benchmark their candidate against what had been revealed there. If they had taken that step, they would have been reminded of their progressive theological perspective and would have posed some questions to explore the theological perspective of their candidate. Had they done so, they would have discovered that he is as clearly conservative as they are clearly progressive, and that therefore he is not a good fit for the church. This benchmarking was not performed.

They called him with all the joy and excitement that is typical of a new pastoral relationship. It was not long before the theological chasm between the pastor and the congregation began to be realized. Conflict developed. Two years later the presbytery was asked to intervene. The presbytery appointed a theologically diverse panel to meet with the congregation in order to illustrate how different theological positions can interact constructively in a church. It was no use. Within a few months, the pastor moved on to another call.

What happened here is a good illustration of the church's lack of experience with evidence-based discernment. At critical junctures, leaders tend to regress to the familiar pattern of a discernment process that is entirely impression-based. In call processes, committees often make their call based more or less on the *chemistry* of the interaction, which is totally out of balance with the *insight* revealed in their organizational intelligence. As a result, churches and pastors often end up in pastoral relationships that do not work well for either side of the covenant.

Such missteps are extremely expensive in every sense of the word. When one considers decreased giving from conflicted members, relocation costs, medical and mental health costs for the pastor, and the impact on other staff positions, the financial impact easily ranges into the hundreds of thousands of dollars. As energy and resources are diverted to dealing with the conflict, important ministry and mission opportunities are missed. Congregational morale takes a real beating. Depending upon the nature of the pastoral contract, the poor fit can go on for years. In that time some congregations will drop below the threshold of affording a full-time pastor and most of these will never recover.

Organizational Intelligence and Pastoral Fit

One promise of organizational intelligence that is integrated into an evidence-based discernment process is that it can help search committees and denominational authorities extend calls that are a better fit between pastor and people. Again, organizational intelligence does not guarantee a positive result, but the lack of it (or, as we have seen, the failure to pay attention to it) almost certainly guarantees a high percentage of unwelcome surprises in the call process.

What can organizational intelligence help specify in determining a candidate who is a good fit for a particular church? It can address the following five areas: subject matters of interest, context, critical abilities, leadership style, and core motivation. Once a search committee specifies what it needs in those five areas, it has the criteria required to evaluate candidates for the position. Next, a committee must shape an interview process that will elicit the appropriate information from candidates to help them evaluate the fit as measured again by the criteria they developed in the previous step.

Subject Matters of Interest

What must a good-fit pastor for this church be interested in?

- A pastor who is a good fit for a church does not have to share the precise theological perspective of the congregation, but does need to appreciate the theological perspectives that are present. How do we know what a person appreciates? The best predictor of future behavior is past behavior. If I know the kinds of books a person has read in the past, it is a good predictor of what he or she will read in the future and suggest what he or she has an appreciation for. What has the candidate been reading?
- A pastor who is a good fit for a church needs to be resonant with the dynamics of the church's size. A family-sized church (under 50 in worship) is a different animal from a pastor-sized church (50 to 150 in worship), is also different from a program-sized church (150 to 350 in worship), is also different from a resource-sized church (over 350 in worship). A pastor who is a good fit for one sized church will be a poor fit for another sized church, even though all the other factors are the same. What are the size dynamics the candidate is most comfortable with?
- A pastor who is a good fit participates in continuing education opportunities that equip leaders with strategies and tactics for the church's culture—Hearth and Home, Paraclete, Magi, Performance. The opportunities and risks for churches exhibiting these different cultures are quite different, and the strategies and tactics that will be

effective in each are different as well. How are these strategies and tactics discovered and honed? With the exception of a few pastor geniuses, they are learned through educational opportunities of one type or another. What has the candidate been learning? What continuing education opportunities has he or she participated in?

Context

What are the circumstances of the work that a good-fit pastor would need to be comfortable with?

- A regionally based or a neighborhood-based church?
- A community population that is growing, stable, in decline?
- A community income that is growing, stable, in decline?
- A theological perspective that is conservative, moderate, progressive, diverse?
- A culture that is Hearth and Home, Paraclete, Magi, or Performance?
- A congregation that evaluates how they feel about the church overall based upon the pastor, power, or ministries?
- A church that is in recovery, chaos, transformation, or stasis?
- A church where the giving level is low with high additional capacity, moderate with moderate additional capacity, high with low additional capacity?

Critical Abilities

What must a good-fit pastor love doing and also do well?

- Abilities that will help the church address the priorities important to members
- Abilities that will help the church make progress on the critical success factors (what members wish the church could do better)
- Abilities that will help the church address issues related to its current level of energy and satisfaction

Leadership Style

How would a good-fit pastor lead this church?

- By excelling at providing direct services, developing a team of lay leaders to run programs, recruiting and managing a staff team?
- By instituting little change, moderate change, high levels of change?

Core Motivation

What will keep a good-fit pastor motivated in this church over the long haul?

- Enjoying direct interactions with people and different ways of serving them?
- Or enjoying the process of helping lay leaders grow and develop?

- Or enjoying the process of being "on stage" and managing a team of professionals?

Armed with this level of organizational intelligence and trained in a solid, behaviorally based interviewing technique, churches and pastors who are a good fit have a fighting chance of finding one another and entering into a shared ministry that bears fruit for the kingdom of God.

Once a pastor is called, the work of an evidence-based succession process is not over. A solid start-up plan is necessary to close the loop. Organizational intelligence is so critical to that component of a succession process that it deserves its own chapter.

Discussion Questions

1. Spend some time talking with others about the pastoral transition history of the last thirty years of your church. Which were the best transitions? Which were the worst ones? What factors made the difference between the good and the not-so-good?

2. This chapter suggests that the succession process in a church should be tailored to the characteristics of the church as disclosed through organizational intelligence. Can you imagine a point in your history where organizational intelligence would have made a significant difference in the pastoral transition process?

3. Pastors are usually selected through a combination of geometry (Is the person a good fit for who we are?) and chemistry (Do we feel good about the person as we interact?). Do you think one is more important than the other? How good a job do does your church do in equipping search committees with organizational intelligence to know what type of person is a good fit for you?

CHAPTER 12

The Start-Up Plan for Succession

Every thing must have a beginning and that beginning
must be linked to something that went before.
—Mary Shelley, English author, 1791–1851

The third component of an evidence-based succession process, following the transition plan and the search plan, which were the focus of the previous chapter, is the start-up plan. The purpose of the start-up plan is to set the course for the new pastor on a positive trajectory.

At start-up, every pastor is on a steep learning curve. To this point, the relationship with the congregation has been largely mediated through a call committee that may or may not characterize the congregation at large. While the congregation has only one subject to learn about, the pastor has hundreds. He or she has so much more to learn than names and faces, though that is challenging enough. The new pastor also must learn who is related to whom, where the relational fault lines run, and how the informal communication network is wired. First impressions can be difficult to reverse. Understanding what is important to the body as a whole and sending a clear, early message that you are in touch with what is important to them is crucial. There is no substitute for learning where the power lies, who holds it . . . and who does not.

A Typical Start-Up Story

The first church I served was a small, rural community in western New York. It was one of only two churches in a thirty-six-square-mile township with a total population of about two thousand people. The church documents listed about fifty people in worship, and after I arrived a few of the older members began to express concerns that they would not be able to pay me. As it turned out, their fears never materialized. Seven years later the church had grown to about two hundred people in worship, acquired additional property on both sides of the building, expanded its programming, and tripled its revenue.

All this sounds good, but there were moments of high anxiety at the beginning that, in reflection, were largely caused by an absence of organizational intelligence. One of the elders, who had been the clerk of session for years and a close friend of three of the previous pastors, did not care for my preaching or the direction I was taking the church. Tension built over the first few months until, finally, he asked me to pay him a visit at his home. After the exchange of country courtesies, he made a clear demand.

"I have the power to make your life difficult in this community," he threatened, "and if you don't change your message, I will do just that."

I describe it as a paradoxical moment in my life when I had an aerobic heartbeat while physically paralyzed in a chair. I believe I did the right thing at that moment, what any pastor would do: I held my ground while trying to understand what was going on underneath. However, it was a period of high anxiety for me because I did not know

- how many people he was relationally connected to in the church.
- how many people looked to him for advice and would be influenced by his counsel.
- what the financial impact would be if he stopped giving.
- how many people in the church were connected to other leaders who were strong enough to weather the storm.
- how strong the church was before I arrived. Was I risking the demise of a small family church or was I liberating them to become something larger?
- the most important factors for determining how members felt about the church overall. Was it the pastor? Was it power? Was it ministry? Was it conflict?
- what members' real priorities for the future were.
- where the church as a whole was theologically.
- where the church as a whole was in its level of flexibility.

I had answers to these questions as they pertained to the views of the search committee, but I was not sure of the answers from the entire church. Over the years that followed, I learned the answers to all those questions. For me, and I believe for many other pastors starting a new call, it would have been helpful to have that information at the beginning. This is another promising aspect of organizational intelligence, giving pastors the information they need to start not only well but confidently.

Winning the People on the Fence

When a new pastor arrives to take the call to a typical church, roughly half the members are clearly satisfied with things at the church. Since they are going to give a new pastor the benefit of the doubt, there is usually not much a pastor can do to lose their support. On the other end of the scale, just under 10 percent of the members are clearly dissatisfied. There is probably not much that can be done about that group either. In any church a small group of people is resolutely dissatisfied.

However, just over 40 percent of the members in a typical church are sitting on the fence. As the metaphor implies, the top of a fence is an inherently unstable place to sit. A relatively small push will cause folks to fall in one direction or the other. Wouldn't it be helpful to know some genie who could tell a new pastor what it is in people's minds that might help them move to the positive side?

The bad news is that there is no genie, but the good news is that organizational intelligence can provide a new pastor with exactly that information. For example, let's say Pastor Mary stands up to preach her first sermon. There are two hundred people in worship. The organizational intelligence has told her that about eighty of those people are on the fence when it comes to how they feel about the church. It has also told her that the three strongest factors making the people on the fence less satisfied with the church are

- the pastor's ability to bring out the best in people,
- the flexibility of the Christian education ministry for people with complex lifestyles, and
- the level of care the church shows for people in times of personal need.

Mary finds a way to touch on each of these areas in her first sermon, and in so doing lets people know that these are on her radar screen. That's what is most important in those early weeks. It is not providing all the answers or developing full-fledged programs. It is demonstrating awareness. For the next four weeks she preaches on personal giftedness and promises a class in the fall that will help folks identify their gifts. That begins to address the first factor, the pastor's ability to bring out the best in people.

Early on, she invests in building a relationship with the Christian formation team. Together they look for creating an online meeting for people whose schedules do not allow them to participate in many activities in church. It is easy to set up and easy for folks to attend in other locations. Thirty people participate in that meeting and they generate lots of ideas. That begins to address the second factor, the flexibility of the Christian education ministry for complex lifestyles.

Finally, Mary announces in worship that she would like to have some folks go with her when she does hospital calling and asks for volunteers. This serves several purposes. First, it gives people a chance to get to know her and is a motivating factor for involvement. Second, it models shared ministry. Third, it signals that the pastor is concerned for people in times of need. Fourth, it helps Mary identify a pool of people who might form the core of a calling ministry that she will develop later.

None of these steps takes a lot of additional work. Mary has to preach and make hospital calls anyway. Online meetings don't require room reservations, setup, copies, or refreshments. They can be recorded and posted on the website for others to view. Without a lot of work, Mary has signaled to the people on the fence that she is aware of what is important to them, leaving an early impression that folks will not soon forget.

Sidestepping the Urgent but Less Important

Paul started as the new pastor at Westbridge Community Church. He had been put on notice in advance of his first worship team meeting that one major item on the agenda had to do with purchasing the new denominational hymnal that had recently hit the market. In order to promote early sales, the publisher was offering a 40 percent discount on purchases made in the next thirty days. The committee was pushing to get this decision made so that the new books could be in the pews by Advent.

Paul looked at the organizational intelligence and gained the following insights:

- Worship and music constitute one of the church's greatest strengths. Members rank the quality of the worship experience higher than 90 percent of the churches in our database.
- For folks sitting on the fence, worship is an important issue regarding how they feel about the church.

- Music is not a critical success factor in the church. People do not have desires for the music ministry that are not being fulfilled.
- Music as an area where members want additional energy invested is unusually low.
- The average giving level in the church is 3.3 percent, which puts the church near capacity, that is, they are unlikely to give much more than they currently give. Even with the 40 percent discount, the purchase of five hundred new hymnals would really put pressure on the church budget right now.

None of these factors argues against purchasing new hymnals in the long term, and Paul has proven in the past with his new congregation that he is not averse to exercising leadership. However, a misstep here could have significant repercussions that he has not yet built the relational capital to handle. Besides, there are a number of issues revealed by the organizational intelligence that indicate action on his part will almost certainly have a significant positive impact on his ministry in the church, and he does not want to get distracted from those issues. Paul concludes that the position he needs to take is to request that the committee delay the decision for a year to give him an opportunity to build support and even identify potential funders.

These two examples illustrate that organizational intelligence not only helps start-up pastors know what to focus on first, it also provides them with a way to discern what needs to be delayed. This strategic deferment is critical to a pastor's success. Without it, a pastor will become set in a reactive mode that will blur his or her strategic focus and make it difficult to accomplish anything significant in the long term.

Relational Networks as Organizational Intelligence

Any effective leader realizes that relationships are the way that things get done in an organization. In a church, relationships have the power to

- get you an appointment in someone's busy calendar.
- catalyze and attract resources (time, talent, money) to new endeavors.
- mobilize a critical mass of people in support of a project.
- hold detractors in check who otherwise might sabotage what you are trying to accomplish.

Relationships, not administration, are the key to long-term efficiency. Many leaders have learned the painful lesson of actions taken by majority vote in a board meeting that never bear fruit, because the pastor has not yet built the relationships to actually get things done.

A comment made to the wrong person in a relational network that was invisible to the pastor can have embarrassing consequences when that message makes its way to an unintended audience. Yet it is precisely this type of organizational intelligence about the relational network that the pastor usually does not have at start-up. What's more, since most pastors have never seen relational network data, it is hard for them to know what they are missing or to realize the value of it when they first see it.

Two researchers at the University of Kentucky have developed a software package called NetDraw that puts this information within reach of church leaders. It uses a very simple assessment instrument that asks for the following information:

- What is your name? (Answered by selecting from a drop-down list of church members.)
- Please list up to ten persons with whom you have a one-on-one relationship and would be comfortable asking for advice. (Also answered by selecting from a drop-down list of church members.)

The assessment instrument is sent to members just prior to the arrival of a new pastor and members are asked to complete it as an act of hospitality and welcome so that the new pastor can get to know the church family. The program NetDraw then generates a series of maps that are provided to the new pastor confidentially. Five of those maps are listed below:

The Congregation Structure Map provides an overview of the relational network of a congregation.

The Isolates Map identifies individuals with no indicated relational connection to other members of the congregation.

The Bridges Map identifies people who connect individuals or groups to one another.

The Islands Map identifies groups of people who are connected to one another but not to the main network of the congregation.

The Central Figures Map identifies the people in the church who have large relational networks.

There is not space here to go over each of these maps in detail, so I will focus on two.

An example of the Congregation Structure Map can be found in figure 12. 1. All the names have been removed from this map so that it can be shared with the congregation. It has little practical value except as a teaching tool to introduce folks to the complexity of the relational system a pastor walks into at start-up.

- The circles are called *nodes*. Each node represents a person.
- Lines connecting the nodes represent indicated relationships.
- Gray nodes represent *isolates*, that is, people where no relationship with others in the church is indicated.
- Black nodes represent *bridge people*. Bridge people are the glue holding everyone else together. Without them, the network fragments into scores of disconnected groups and individuals.

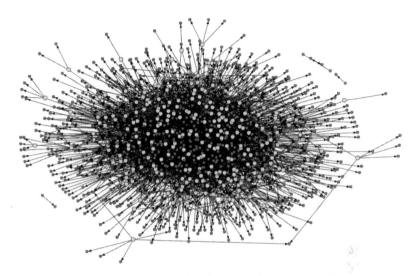

Figure 12.1. The Congregation Structure Map, Anywhere Church

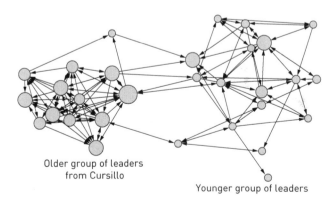

Older group of leaders
from Cursillo

Younger group of leaders

Figure 12.2. The Central Figures Map, Anywhere Church
(names have been removed for purposes of this book)

The second map, figure 12.2, is an example of the Central Figures Map. Since the names are typically retained on the Central Figures Map, this one is shared with the pastor confidentially. Another new feature has been added to this map: the size of the node is proportionate to the number of people who named him or her as a person with whom they have a one-on-one relationship and would be comfortable asking for advice. Most of the nodes have been removed from this map. Only the larger ones remain.

This is a map of the people who members indicate are most influential in the system. Notice that in this church there are two groups of influential people. The first group (on the left) is an older group of leaders that in the 1980s shared an experience called Cursillo. The second group (on the right) represents a younger group of leaders who have joined the church in the last twenty years. They are less tightly connected. The strength of the connections is determined by how often people name one another on their list of "people with whom I have a one-on-one relationship and would be comfortable asking for advice." It is indicated by the density of the lines connecting the nodes. The more lines, the stronger the network.

And I'm Not the Only One Who Feels This Way

Let's look at an example of how these maps can assist a new pastor. Pastor Joan has just moved into her office at New Brunswick Church and is putting her books away when she hears a knock on the door. She opens it to a woman in her forties who is obviously distressed and asks for a moment to talk. Pastor Joan motions her in.

Her guest immediately begins to lay out a number of concerns that she has about the church, ranging from worship to child care. She has been eagerly waiting for Pastor Joan to arrive so that she could share her concerns. It has been months since the church has had a pastor that she felt comfortable with. Several times in the conversations she punctuates her concerns with the statement "And I'm not the only one who feels this way. There are lots of forty-year-olds in this church who feel very differently about things than everyone else."

As she leaves, Pastor Joan pulls out her file of organizational intelligence and looks at the Central Figures Map. The guest who just left her office is not on it. Obviously, this does not mean that she is not entitled to pastoral care and attention to her concerns. However, it does mean that it is less likely that Pastor Joan has a *corporate pastoral concern* to deal with. When she checks other intelligence reports on the church she sees that the church is in the transformational quadrant. Finally, when she looks at the goals for folks in their forties and fifties, she notes that they are not substantially different from older and younger members.

Pastor Joan takes a moment, prays again for her guest, and finishes unpacking her books.

Most seasoned pastors know that the people who visit them in their first weeks of ministry at a new call have an agenda that may not necessarily be in the best interest of the church. Good intuition combined with organizational intelligence can work hand in glove in helping the new pastor be more confident making that call.

Your First Ninety Days (or Thirty Meals Out)

If you, as the arriving pastor, knew the names of the thirty people in the church who are best positioned to help move the church forward under your leadership, what would you do? I would imagine that you would want to make sure that you connect with them in a systematic, intentional way soon after your arrival. I call this the first Thirty Meals Out Plan.

There is no question that *every* person in the body of Christ is a child of God and deserves to be nourished, nurtured, sheltered, and engaged in ministry by the church to which they belong. The best way to insure that the church will provide those ministries to members is through the pastor's work in developing a team of committed and respected leaders who will provide support, time, and resources for that effort. And that requires relationships.

Some will be formal leaders, that is, folks in official positions of power such as boards, committees, ministry teams, and staff. Some will be informal leaders who hold no office but still are influential within the congregation. The Central Figures Map helps a new pastor identify the folks held in highest regard in the congregation. With this organizational intelligence in hand, a pastor can intentionally seek these people out over the first ninety days of his or her ministry (or first thirty meals out) and begin to build the relationships that can serve and strengthen the church over the entire tenure of the pastor.

Discussion Questions

1. Can mistakes be made on the part of a new pastor that are difficult to recover from? What has been the process that your church leadership has used to help a new pastor start on a positive trajectory with your congregation? How important do you think it is for a new pastor to know the vitality status, the member focus, the critical success factors, the level

of criticality (one of the most important tasks for the leadership to focus on), and the organizational culture of the church?

2. Let's say that Pastor Jones begins her ministry in a church where the relational maps show five cliques, that is, five groups of people that are islands to themselves without any connections to the other groups. Is that important information for Pastor Jones? Given that information, how might Pastor Jones begin her work?

3. When organizational intelligence discloses some significant issues in a church, how should that information be shared with pastoral candidates?
   - Share all information with all candidates for the position.
   - Share more information with candidates as it becomes clearer that they would be a good fit for the church and there is interest on both sides.
   - Withhold some of the "negative" information for fear that it might drive a good candidate away.
   - Share little organizational intelligence. Let the person discover the information on his or her own.

PART 4

Integration into Faith and Practice

CHAPTER 13

Information, Meaning, and Creativity

*What we see is largely dependent upon what we were thinking
before we looked.*

—Source unknown

T he work of the Spirit is often revealed not by information itself but by how we choose to arrange it. Shortly after my wife and I moved into our present apartment, we bought a large clock that we placed over the fireplace. At the same time we hung a sconce with the same color palette on an adjacent wall. A few weeks later we were sitting on the sofa when I looked over at the sconce, cocked my head, and blurted out, "You know, I don't think that sconce goes there."

"I don't either," she concurred. "How hard would it be to take it down?"

"Not that hard," I answered.

Then a thought went through my head in precisely these words: "If that sconce falls off the wall in the next twenty-four hours, we will know for sure that it doesn't belong there."

The next day my wife was taking a nap on the same sofa. I was in an adjacent chair working on my computer. Suddenly, a crash caused her to bolt upright and yell, "What was that?" I looked over by the fireplace and sure enough, the sconce had fallen off the wall, pulling off plaster and scattering votive candles and their holders across the floor. It had been hanging there undisturbed for six weeks.

That startling event occurred on the very same day that my wife unexpectedly came across a medal that her father had given her the year before he had died that she thought had been lost for good. Within an hour of that discovery, she located a DVD with photos of grandchildren that we also thought was gone. We had conducted several extensive, fruitless searches for both of these items in the previous few weeks. It led me to contemplate the meaning of these three unusual events that all happened within a few hours of one another. I believe that I know the answer to that question, but I need to take action to know for sure.

The process I have just described grouped events by meaning. Three apparently disconnected events, none of which caused the others, occurred close enough to one another in time to trigger my search for an underlying pattern. Carl Jung called this "grouping of events by meaning" *synchronicity*. Working with physicist Wolfgang Pauli, Jung constructed a theory by which individual consciousness is shifted from an egocentric viewpoint to one that is more holistic and universal by observing these spiritual "coincidences."

The work of the Spirit is often disclosed when we group information by meaning. The Bible is chock-full of accounts of God's guidance that occur as a grouping of information or events by meaning. In Exodus, at the very same time that Pharaoh's army is about to catch up with the children of Israel, they arrive at the sea, just as a strong wind begins to blow (Exod. 14:21). In Acts, at the very same time that some Gentiles are looking for Peter, he is having a "vision" of creepy animals he is told to eat and at the very same time is trying to figure out how to live out the commission of the resurrected, now ascended Jesus (10:11). In the book of Esther (4:14), Queen Esther is challenged to connect her place in time with the need of her people, with the words "And who knows whether you have not come to the kingdom for such a time as this?" If those words do not send a shiver of purpose through the soul of a church (or at least the longing for it), nothing will. It is instructive, and somewhat surprising, to leaf through the Bible and discover how much of it can be seen through the lens of grouping events and information by meaning.

Two Ways of Grouping Information

Information can be grouped in two ways: by cause and by meaning. Organizational assessment groups information by cause, or likely cause.

It looks at energy and satisfaction levels in a congregation and seeks to understand the factors that are driving it. It seeks to gauge what is important to members on the assumption that by improving their experience along those lines the church will discover a new zest and vitality. It hopes to uncover aspects of organizational culture that might suggest one course of action will be more likely to succeed than another. It explores what has been learned from the larger body of Christ to identify possible failure paths as well as best practices. The assumption that lies beneath it all is that better information leads to better decisions, with results that are potentially more fruitful and durable. This is the advantage of grouping information by cause or likely cause.

The second way of grouping information is by meaning; that is, connecting information or events to one another because they disclose an underlying pattern, not because they have caused one another. In a passage of my life that I have described in detail elsewhere, I founded a project for abandoned HIV children in Honduras called Montana de Luz. Many of the key elements in the success of that project can be described by grouping information and events by cause. Get clear about vision, build a base of support, plan and execute an effective fund-raising approach, and so forth. When we group information and events by cause, we tend to focus on methods that have been found to be effective.

However, that is only half the story. At critical junctures, it was a grouping of events and information by meaning that was decisive for moving forward. Permit me to illustrate. The session of the church I pastored made a weekend retreat every fall to discern directions for the next year. In November 1998, they discerned that the church was being called to invest more of its resources in serving those outside the church. Their one stipulation was that any externally focused ministries needed to provide members a way to get personally engaged rather than to simply send money.

Two clusters of events would soon change my life forever.

One month later we went to my parents' home for Christmas dinner. My sister and brother-in-law brought along a guest, a young Honduran named Paul Mendez. I was intrigued by the stories he told about his homeland. At the end of the evening he shook my hand and said, "You should come to Honduras."

In other situations, I probably would have thanked him politely for the generous invitation and said good-bye. Yet, I could not help but group my meeting with Paul Mendez and the session retreat by meaning. What did it mean that one month after this session retreat where leaders had discerned a distinct call, I had this unusual and unexpected meeting with a Honduran inviting me to his country? It was that grouping of information by meaning that was the critical factor in the development of a home for children with HIV in Honduras, not a set of causal connections or a particular method.

The second cluster of events was tragic in nature. Three students from the local high school killed themselves over a period of a few months, two of them within weeks of the session retreat. Those deaths launched me into suicide prevention work, training thousands of people and helping develop statewide and countrywide suicide prevention plans. Here again, it was the grouping of information by meaning that thrust me into engagement, not a simple chain of cause and effect.

Wholeness requires that church leaders and members develop the capacity to group information by both cause and meaning. It also requires that they develop the capacity to take action steps using both cause and meaning, for it is the combination that leads to energy and zest for their purpose on the earth. Using one without the other leads to a spiritual malnutrition of the Christian body. Using another analogy, it flattens a multidimensional universe onto a two-dimensional veneer. God has given us two eyes to represent these two different ways of seeing. When we choose one to the exclusion of the other, we create the distortions represented by the Cyclops of ancient mythology, who had a single eye in the middle of his forehead.

To avoid becoming that Cyclops, we need the intelligence provided by assessment tools, the first eye, combined with an inspired plan to move toward greater health, the second eye. A church assessment tool is a stethoscope; its listens for the heart. You do not get a stronger heart by using more stethoscopes and you do not strengthen a heart simply by listening to it. A stronger heart is the result of exercises that have been designed to strengthen the cardiovascular system. These are different in kind; they look nothing like a stethoscope. Both work together to produce vitality.

People who can group information only by cause can be conceptually agile. People who can group information only by meaning can be deep and insightful. Wisdom consists in understanding both ways of seeing, knowing when to use one rather than the other, and possessing the capacity to weave them together. My objective is to reflect on what an evidence-based discernment process might look like that incorporates the two ways of seeing that I have just described.

Decoding the Evidence through Discernment

First, an evidence-based discernment process proposes that the Holy Spirit is attempting to break into our corporate lives as churches with messages that will help and guide us. This is an expression of the kingdom of God already breaking into the world that Jesus announced in his proclamation. Our goal is to understand or decode those messages. If this were not the case, it would not be a discernment process.

Second, an evidence-based process proposes that the messages the Spirit brings to churches are designed to help them become fruitful in their life and ministries. This can be expressed in the Old Testament through the Ezekiel vision of water flowing out from under the threshold of the temple and into the world, where it turns saltwater into freshwater. It can be expressed in the New Testament vision of a tree known by its fruit and the command of Jesus that we bear fruit that abides.

Third, an evidence-based discernment process proposes that while organizational intelligence can help leaders become clear about where the church is, what is important to members, and what are potential failure paths and best practices, leaders must also attend to grouping information and experiences by meaning. Groupings would include but not be limited to the convergence of the following:

> Scripture readings
> Sermons
> Meditations
> Dreams
> Images
> Events in the community and world
> Impressions
> Journaling

At its best, organizational intelligence helps create a heightened psychological state that opens the soul to these other sources of meaning. Sometimes organizational intelligence discloses that the familiar ways will not lead the church forward. In the crisis this creates, leaders may temporarily regress to behaviors of a previous spiritual stage of the discernment process. The promise of that moment is the possibility that the crisis will eventually lift them to a higher level of development that gives them a "second eye" and transforms the universe into a multidimensional reality in which their purpose is being revealed.

Fourth, given the fact that many leaders are new to the approach, an evidence-based discernment process proposes that churches and individuals must develop their capacity to discern what the Spirit is saying to them and that they can become better with practice. If there is growth in our ability to discern the leading of the Spirit, then there should be some evidence to that effect. Using the metaphor of water and fruit for vitality and transformation, if the water flows in a trickle or the fruit is sparse and withered, it suggests that we have room to grow in our discernment.

Fifth, an evidence-based discernment process proposes that that there are concrete ways of measuring the fruitfulness of a discernment process through the witness of members. In this model, the primary evidence for the vitality of a congregation is the level of satisfaction and energy members bear witness to in the church. Regardless of the particular theological persuasion of a congregation, its mission, or its vision, it will bear little fruit if people are restive and mechanical in their shared life. Churches moving deeper into the transformational quadrant are more likely to be growing numerically, but even if they are not, numeric growth is a realistic and achievable option for them. It is not an option for churches where their discernment processes are leading deeper and deeper into the recovery quadrant.

If a course of action is not leading to higher levels of energy and satisfaction, it suggests that members, leaders, or both are not correctly interpreting the messages coming to them from the Holy Spirit, and that additional growth is necessary.

Organizational Intelligence and Spirituality

It often surprises people that a person so committed to the role of organizational intelligence in discernment should also advocate a spirituality with mystical components. The reaction is simply a testament to the modern mindset that cannot integrate opposites. Unfortunately, the church has bitten deeply into this apple and is yet to be kissed back into consciousness.

When I was starting the mission project in Honduras, I served for a time as a mission specialist on staff of a large church. Having stepped out of the father role of senior pastor and into the brother role of an associate, people would confide in me, telling me stories that they would not share with the senior pastor. I conducted a small research project during this time that consisted of a single question: Have you ever had an important spiritual experience that you have never shared with anyone in the church for fear that they would think you are weird?

The answer was consistently "Yes."

Then they would pause, look from one side to the other, lower their voice, and tell me the story. And incredible stories they were!

The reality is that most churches do not do a good job systematically developing either their leaders or their members to integrate intelligence and experiences of meaning into actionable steps that lead to greater zest and vitality. Today, we need all the individuals and churches full of zest and vitality that we can find.

Organizational Intelligence and Creativity

The major point of this book is that organizational intelligence holds promise for leaders today that is largely untapped. Another way of saying this is that leaders expect too little from the information that can be readily generated as a result of the revolution in Internet technology, and they are largely unaware of its possibilities.

On the other hand, leaders can also expect too much of organizational intelligence. To be fruitful, organizational intelligence must not only be interwoven with a robust spiritual practice but also explored with a lively creativity. This is true of any technological advance.

In 1984 a lay leader approached me with the question, "Would you like to have a computer on your desk?" In retrospect, my response was somewhat humorous: "What would I do with a computer on my desk?" It was difficult for me to imagine all the possibilities that the personal computer would open up in my life. As an engineer, I had used a computer many times to do quick calculations with complex formulas. It took me awhile to realize that an element of creativity was required on my part to imagine how I could use a computer on my desk. Once I began to think creatively about the matter, a new day dawned.

I find the same response from folks who are introduced to organizational intelligence in its many different facets. "That's cool!" is often the first response, shortly followed by "What do you do with it?" I attempt in this book to illustrate how organizational intelligence can be useful, specifically in the area of succession planning. But the long answer to the question "What do you do with it?" is that leaders must engage their creative thinking to discover how to apply the new information now made available to them.

The subject of creativity is vast and the literature extensive. I will make no attempt to address it here. However, it is important for leaders to recognize that creativity is required in the application of organizational intelligence. One obstacle may be that leaders are accustomed to dealing with count data that is primarily used to make decisions rather than to formulate solutions and explore new possibilities. Organizational intelligence goes far beyond financial reports, but seeing the information in that familiar form can channel a person down the same, noncreative neural pathways.

What is needed in the church today are "infopreneurs," that is, folks who can take information and think creatively about new ventures or enterprises consistent with the mission and vision of the church. As an example, I am now working in partnership with Kairos and Associates, a ministry that assists churches with financial campaigns. We are in the process of systematically collecting organizational intelligence that will help leaders tailor their financial campaigns based on five factors that are uniquely weighted for a particular church. One thing we are discovering is that for most congregations, with some notable exceptions, the state of the economy is not as big a factor in giving as we thought. More than one leader has looked at the data and exclaimed, "We have got to stop giving people an excuse (the economy is bad) to stop being generous. Let's find some creative ways to focus on faith, hope, and impact!"

Infopreneurs in the church have the gift to make the creative connection between information and application. If we could supply all organizational intelligence with the label "Some Creativity Required," perhaps we would set an expectation that would encourage leaders to look around for those folks in the church that possess the infopreneurial gift.

Other Concerns in the Application of Organizational Intelligence

I have found that the concept of evidence-based discernment raises a number of other concerns. What follows are some of the most common.

I think it is possible for a church to be bearing good fruit even if members who bear witness to that fact are dissatisfied and de-energized. None of the evidence supports that position. Churches in this state are consistently indicating poorer worship experiences, are less invested in spiritual formation and education, are less positive regarding the quality of relationships within the church, and are more likely to be focused on internal issues rather than serving those beyond their walls.

Still, members can be having a positive impact on the world as individuals even when the church is going through a difficult time. Yes. Here we must make a distinction between the practice of individual members and the witness of the church as a whole. As we have seen with spiritual vitality, a church can be full of members with a robust individual spiritual practice and, nonetheless, it is demoralized, conflicted, and fragmented as a body. It is the health and vitality of the church as the body of Christ with which we are concerned. In the long run, it will be difficult to make a case in the world that Christianity is a meaningful option for the human race if members cannot find a way to live in community that is enriching and purposeful.

What about small churches? Isn't it difficult for members to be satisfied and energized in a small church? No. It is difficult for members in a small church to be satisfied and energized if they are living with either facilities or values that carry the burdens of being a larger church. It is always important to remember that somewhere in the United States there are twenty-five people meeting in a home, school, or storefront today that in five years will be a five-hundred-member church. When I was a new Christian and new to a community, we started a Bible study before we even found a church. The energy level in that group was quite high, and we had no pastor, budget, or building. It is a matter of purpose.

Are you concerned that people looking for signs in their lives will go off on wild goose chases that lead nowhere or even get them in trouble? Yes. That is why I propose an evidence-based approach. If a discernment process does not make the church healthier, the evidence reveals this result, and we make adjustments. I am more concerned about impression-based discernment processes that have no way of determining if progress is being made, and, therefore, no signal that changes are required.

I'm all for making decisions based on evidence, but I think we need more objective measures like finances and attendance. There are two problems with financial and attendance data if used alone. First, changes in giving and engagement are usually downstream from changes in satisfaction and energy, sometimes by as much as two or three years. By the time the leadership realizes that something is wrong, it is sometimes too late. Second, giving and engagement evidence do not provide us with insight into the patterns that are affecting how people are perceiving and experiencing the church. Finally, what we measure sends a message to people regarding what we value. As a church, we are called to care for the souls of our people, including what they think and feel, not just their attendance and their money.

From the questions and answers above, you can probably detect that I anticipate the concept of evidence-based discernment will encounter a number of obstacles along the way. We will tackle a number of those in the next chapter.

Discussion Questions

1. Look at the life of your church over the last thirty days. What have been some of the more important events? How would you group those events by cause? How would you group them by meaning? Is your church one where it is easier for people to talk about what caused certain things to happen in the history of the church or is it easier for them to talk about what different events *mean* in the life of the church (how God was acting)?

2. One purpose of organizational intelligence is to help leaders stop wasting time and energy debating what *is* so that they can spend their best energies working on an inspired creativity for what *can be*. What difference would

it make to your leadership team if you could invest a significant amount of energy in creating a future for the church?

3. Have you ever had an important spiritual experience that you have never shared with anyone in the church for fear that they would think you are weird?

CHAPTER 14

Objections to Using Evidenced-Based Discernment

*I'd be glad to give to the United Way. I have just never had
anyone explain it to me that way before.*

—Employee, upon being told by his boss he would be fired if he didn't make a contribution

W hen I was a boy, I noticed (along with thousands of other third grade students) that the continents seemed to fit together. Out of curiosity, I traced the outline of the continents from a world map, cut them out with a pair of scissors, and glued their interlocking coastlines onto a second sheet of paper. When I took my discovery to the teacher and indicated that it looked like the continents once were together, she smiled and said that while that looked to be the case, it was a simple coincidence. Continents don't move. I believed her.

Now, of course, we know that continents do move. Plate tectonics has become a staple of elementary education. It was first proposed by Alfred Wegener in 1912. However, Wegener was not a geologist and his theory was rejected. It was not until geophysicist Jack Oliver provided the seismologic evidence for continental drift in 1968 that Wegener was finally vindicated. At eighteen years of age, I had to change my mind. The continents *do* move.

Evidence-based discernment provides information that sometimes is exactly what we would expect, sometimes confirms hunches that we were not confident enough to act upon, and sometimes totally surprises us. Occasionally we discover that long-held assumptions that we have made about ministry are simply wrong. I have many opinions about the church. In light of the evidence, I have had to change some of them.

Evidence-based discernment is a different way of thinking about how leaders might discern a direction for their church. It is natural to expect that people will not change their minds easily. Important questions need to be answered and concerns addressed. That is the purpose of this chapter. Below I identify and discuss eight common objections to evidence-based discernment.

Objection 1: Technology and Closing the Feedback Loop

First there is the issue of technology. We are all aware that technology has revolutionized the way we live. One impact of technology is that it has closed the feedback loop between those who send messages and those who receive them. Today, when a performer releases a new song, the feedback is nearly instantaneous across a variety of social networking media, including Twitter, Facebook, blogs, IMs, and email. The same is true for those who provide services. I can go online and see how people rate automotive services, beauty salons, schools, financial services, medical services, hotels, pet services, and restaurants.

Churches cannot escape the feedback loop. In the city in which I live, thirty-nine churches are rated online, and the reader can sort them by most reviewed or highest rated. I was conducting focus groups in a regional association a number of months ago. When I asked participants what they would like to see the church do, one young adult referenced a conference where members of the audience were invited to text comments that were posted in real time on a screen behind the speaker. That's closing the feedback loop!

The Christian church has been remarkably effective at harnessing emerging technologies to communicate its message. In 1440 a German named Johannes Gutenberg combined his knowledge of metallurgy with the mechanics of a wine press to produce a technology that would revolutionize the world—the printing press. The church was quick to seize upon the new opportunity to communicate its message to the masses. The first Bible was printed around

1450. By 1499 an estimated fifteen million books had been printed, many of them religious in content. Similarly, the church has capitalized upon digital and Internet technologies to disseminate its message, including email, websites, podcasts, audiovisual productions, radio and television broadcasts, videoconferencing, and webinars. The way the church disseminates information is quite different today than it was five hundred years ago, largely due to the technology it has adopted and adapted to its purposes.

However, when it comes to the way that leaders *receive* information from members as they make decisions—the feedback loop—the church is essentially back in the fifteenth century. Leaders gather around a boardroom table and bring into the discernment process the information they have gleaned from a relatively small number of conversations within their sphere of relationships. Each person extrapolates that information across the entire congregation in order to fill in the blanks of the conversations they have not had.

The question is not whether the church is going to use technology or not. The question is whether the church is going to use technology to listen as well as it uses technology to speak. Corporately, is the church going to be "quick to listen, slow to speak" (James 1:19)? Evidence-based discernment, using technology, provides a way for us to fulfill this biblical mandate to an extent that previously was impossible.

Objection 2: Discernment by Survey

Leaders are sometimes afraid that evidence-based discernment will result in an abdication of leadership, what I call discernment by survey. There is a risk here. If Moses had decided which direction to go in the wilderness by surveying the Israelites, all the Jewish people today would have Egyptian names! Shouldn't leaders be making decisions about the direction of the church without worrying about where people are? Won't organizational intelligence short-circuit the process of listening for where God wants the church to go? I believe these questions confuse leading with commanding.

Both a commander and a leader have a destination in mind. Beyond that, the similarity ceases. A commander issues orders to arrive at a destination in the fastest, most efficient, and most effective way possible, quite independent of the thinking of the people being commanded. This is often because the success of the mission requires rapid, coordinated action that becomes impossible when time must be spent soliciting everyone's views on what they are thinking, how they are feeling, and what to do next. In a crisis situation, a focus on organizational intelligence is not only undesirable, it can be dangerous. Crisis situations require commanders.

A leader, in contrast, develops a way for people to move toward the destination by beginning where they are. A number of years ago, I met a ballroom dance instructor who always began his lessons by having the men simply walk across the floor. After they traversed the thirty-foot room he would simply say to them, "Congratulations, men. If you can walk, you can dance." The secret of his success, and he had success aplenty, was that he began where people were.

Evidence-based discernment is incarnational. It follows the pattern established in Jesus, who brings the kingdom of God into people's lives beginning where they are. Sometimes leaders will discern that they are called to go more or less in the direction that people are already pointed. Other times leaders will discern that they must set the sail in a different direction, even though the wind be across their bow. In those situations, they will make the case for why change is necessary, with the goal of losing as few people as possible in the turning.

Churches where pastors, bishops, and executives are commanding are not doing well today. Most, though not all, are recognizing that the denominational loyalty among members that once positioned them to command is now gone. However, without organizational intelligence, a person who is committed to leading can be inadvertently perceived as commanding because of a miscalculation of the starting point. As they say, "If you are one step ahead of the people, you are leading. If you are two steps ahead, you are being run out of town."

Objection 3: Measurement

A third concern has to do with measurement. "There are some things you can measure and some things you can't," folks say. "You can't measure feelings."

This springs from a confusion of count data with witness data. It is true that you can't measure feelings in the same way that you can count dollars or names on a membership role. You can, however, ask a person to bear witness to them.

As I said earlier, my wife is a hospital emergency department nurse. She can't measure pain in the same way that she takes a blood pressure. She can ask a person to indicate their level of pain on a scale of one to ten. The number symbolizes the level of pain. Even though she can't "see" the pain, the witness of the patient has a significant effect on what she does next. If the answer is two she takes one course of action. If the answer is ten she takes a different course of action.

A church leader can't see pain either. Neither can a leader see love, joy, peace, patience, faith, bliss, dismay, doubt, purpose, fulfillment, hope, inspiration, God's presence, guilt, or shame. In each case, a leader can ask members to bear witness to these realities and to symbolize them in a number. And of all people, Christians should be able to deal with symbols.

Objection 4: Mathematics and Statistics

This leads to a fourth concern, the use of mathematics. As I have said, numbers are a tool that help us get a grasp on things that are otherwise invisible to us, namely, the perspectives, experiences, and aspirations of people. The Hebrews believed that numbers were a gift from God. The number twelve, for example, was considered holy, partly because it was so useful in the marketplace. Even today, it is convenient to have goods sold by the dozen, because you can get half of a dozen, a third of a dozen, a quarter of a dozen, a sixth of a dozen, two thirds of a dozen, or three quarters of a dozen . . . and not have to break a single donut!

I will grant that evidence-based discernment is aided by certain mathematical skills. To determine if those skills are within your grasp, I have constructed a quick, four-question test below. (There are no trick questions here, so don't try too hard.)

1. You will find below the responses of a congregation to the statement, "On the whole, I am satisfied with things in the church." How many people strongly disagreed?

Strongly disagree	8 people
Disagree	14 people
Tend to disagree	24 people
Tend to agree	55 people
Agree	102 people
Strongly agree	32 people

2. What is the average of the following four numbers?

    3 4 6 7

3. Look at the following series of 10 numbers. Locate the number six. How many of the numbers in the series are less than six?

    1 2 3 4 5 6 7 8 9 1 0

4. Look at the two columns of numbers below. Do you see a pattern?

Column A	Column B
1	2
2	4
3	6

If your answers to the questions were "8 people," "5," "5," and "yes," then you have the mathematical aptitude required for evidence-based discernment. Next question.

Objection 5: Consumer-Driven Churches

A fifth concern is that if we worry too much about how people in the church are doing (their perceptions, experiences, and aspirations), it will simply accelerate the trend toward an inwardly focused, consumer-driven church where members are preoccupied with their own needs and oblivious to the needs of the world. As we shall see later, the exact opposite appears to be the case. The better members feel about their life within the body of Christ, the more likely they are to focus upon the needs of the world outside the church. This would suggest that one of the best ways to get people engaged in the needs of the world is to develop a church where members give evidence of high levels of satisfaction and energy.

Objection 6: A Focus on Weaknesses

A sixth concern is that evidence-based discernment processes focus people on the weaknesses of the church rather than its strengths. This is a misconception. The starting point of an evidence-based process is the witness that members are making regarding their experiences and their values.

Religious systems across the country are struggling to come up with some definition of health and vitality for their churches. Almost all the criteria that have been developed are externally imposed. One middle judicatory defines health and vitality based upon how a local congregation spends its money, with particular weight upon the percentage of annual receipts that are directed beyond the local church. Some use implicit criteria based upon a local congregation's support of denominational causes, using numbers of participants, dollars, or frequency of engagement (all count data). Though unspoken, the clergy in most regional associations can point out the congregations that are flagship churches in the eyes of denominational executives. However, definitions of health and vitality that are clear, measurable, and witness driven are virtually nonexistent.

An evidence-based discernment process does not begin with an externally imposed standard of health and vitality. It always begins with the witness of members themselves. If members are bearing witness to high levels of satisfaction and energy, those are the definitive indicators of health. If members are bearing witness to low levels of satisfaction and energy, those are the definitive indicators of pain in one form or another. Acknowledging that pain, and the experiences that contribute to it, is an important step in the discernment (and in some cases, therapeutic) process. In addition, evidence-based discernment often reveals unconscious, self-defeating patterns in the culture of a church. Occasionally, underlying problems known only to a few members surface in an evidence-based process. If we skip the step of listening to the witness of members in these areas, we run Jeremiah's risk of "healing the wound lightly."

Once we have heard the witness of members regarding their perspectives, experiences, and aspirations; once we have discovered the implicit patterns of these perspectives, experiences, and aspirations; once members have discovered who they are in relationship to the rest of the body of Christ, any number of methods can be used to help leaders complete the discernment process. I tend to favor health-based approaches that look for reservoirs of energy that can fuel healing, renewal, and growth. However, it is important to stay close to the experiences and values of the members. Evidence-based discernment ultimately requires that we focus on what is important to those we are serving. Identifying strengths that do not address the issues that are critical to achieving what is important to members misses the mark.

Perhaps an example will help clarify this point. Members of a church I will call St. Anywhere bear witness to being demoralized; they indicate they are both unhappy and out of energy. In addition, they bear witness to being theologically conservative and to a culture that values stability, consistency, familiarity, and clarity. They exhibit an implicit pattern of being clergy-focused. The peer evidence across the church is clear: theologically conservative churches that value a high level of stability are virtually always unhappy and out of energy.

The leaders of St. Anywhere bear witness to the fact that it is important to them that the church regains a higher level of vitality and excitement about its mission. In order to achieve what is most important to the members, the church must increase its missional flexibility; that is, it must find ways to adapt in order to become more effective in achieving its mission. With this organizational intelligence in hand, the leaders can begin to explore times in the past when the church has been able to do just that. A positive line of inquiry may identify past behaviors and experiences that can build confidence and offer guidance on how to move forward in a strength-based manner.

However, not just any strength will do! If strengths are identified and reinforced that will not help the church achieve what members identify as most important to them, more harm than good has been done. The promise of an evidence-based discernment process is that it will help leaders focus on strengths that will help the church achieve what is most important to its members, rather than inadvertently reinforce behaviors that in the short term may feel positive and affirming but in the long term lead to an undesired destination.

Objection 7: I Already Know What's Going On in This Church

A seventh concern that is sometimes voiced by denominational executives or other outside consultants goes something like this: "I already know what is going on in this church. I don't need additional evidence to tell me that." Sometimes, this is absolutely true. An astute individual with a history of engagement with the congregations in a region may have 20/20 insight into what is going on in a particular congregation. Even if that is the case, the executive is in the position of having to both deliver his 20/20 diagnosis and provide guidance on how to move forward. As we have already seen, most church leaders are not clear regarding their members' perceptions, experiences, and aspirations (though they generally believe they are). This means that leaders will have to yield to the opinion of a person who is not regularly involved in their church, whose office is some miles away, whom they may never have met before, and who is associated with an organization that, on the whole, has the lowest level of satisfaction of any nonprofit institution we have researched (about 30 percent on average).[1] Organizational intelligence frees the consultant from having to spend his or her influential capital on the diagnostic side so that it can be invested on the strategic and tactical side, where it is most important.

Objection 8: Too Focused on Success

Finally, there is a concern that an evidence-based discernment process will lead to a focus on "success." I was raised in an era of a declining church buttressed by the mantra "We are not called to be successful. We are called to be faithful." Like most simplistic dichotomies, this one obscures an alternative synthesis that is much more promising: "We are called to be faithful and fruitful." If a particular line of faithful action is not bearing fruit in terms of count data (numbers of people, dollars, frequency) or witness data (love, joy, peace, patience, kindness, and so forth), both Scripture and good sense require that we reconsider our course. Similarly, if a particular line of fruitful action is violating core values of our faith (justice, mercy, courage, witness, integrity), we must reconnoiter our journey.

From a business standpoint, no other organization (short of a monopoly) has the luxury of indifference to the effectiveness (ineffectiveness) of its practices. When churches plead for exemption from this accountability, they not only sentence themselves to stagnation and malaise but they also separate themselves from the daily experiences of their parishioners, who must live in a world where impact matters. When leaders object with statements like, "I won't have my church turned into a Walmart," they are missing the fact that the church should at least be as good as any commercial enterprise in fulfilling its mission. In fact, it should be better. No organization in the world should outperform the church in offering to its people a sense of belonging, purpose, and meaning. This is a call to our birthright.

Leaders who understand the importance of both faithfulness and fruitfulness welcome the guidance provided by an evidence-based discernment process. Who wants to waste time going down a path that is increasingly barren? Evidence is derived not only from organizational intelligence but also from personal intelligence, that is, intelligence about an individual's life, gifts, and motivations. An evidence-based process can help illuminate a misfit between a pastor and a church so that both can move on in other, more promising directions. In other cases, evidence-based discernment can help a pastor stay steady at the helm when it indicates that he or she is precisely what a church needs for its long-term renewal and the short-term pain is simply a necessary blip on the screen.

A final question might be posed: Why now? The church has functioned for years without an emphasis on organizational intelligence. What has changed? The answer to that question is the subject of the next chapter.

Discussion Questions

1. Tell about a time when you had to change your mind about something important. What was it that changed your mind? How did you go about letting people know that you had changed your mind?

2. Which objections in this chapter are most significant to you? How well does the chapter address that objection?

3. Which objections in this chapter are most likely to be raised by members of your leadership team or congregation? What other concerns may need to be addressed?

CHAPTER 15

Information-Seeking and Organizational Stages

It is the theory that decides what we can observe.
—Albert Einstein, quoted in Heisenberg, *Physics and Beyond,* 1971

The rabbit's eye differs from that of the owl.
—Greek proverb

The thoughtful reader will recognize that the enterprise of evidence-based discernment represents a major shift in how religious bodies chart their course. The shift affects not only local church leaders but also regional associations and national bodies.

As I write this chapter, the phone rings. A man introduces himself to me and follows up quickly by saying, "I am a member of a church that ... well .. . isn't going anywhere. At least I don't think it is. Our pastor is a nice enough guy. In fact, I really like him. When I talk with him about an assessment of where we are as a church, he says it is not really possible. I don't know. It just seems that after ten years there must be *some* way to get an idea where things stand. Do you have anything that can help us?"

I receive calls like this one on a regular basis. Using his own words, what he is asking for is organizational intelligence. His gut tells him that it must

	Instrumental Stage	Generalizing Stage	Neural Stage	Integrating Stage
Values	Loyalty Position Command and control Internal resources	Affiliations Alliances Tenure	Buy-in Timely decisions	Transparency Effectiveness Experimentation External resources
Is effective in these contexts	Mono-optional cultures Cultural-religious alliance Short-term crisis	Small communities Homogeneous populations Stable environments	Diverse communities Multioptional cultures Leadership transitions Long-term crisis management	Rapidly changing environments Learning cultures Effective "outliers"
Seeks information by . . .	Count data: members, money, facilities	Conversational data Information from episodic interactions Corporate memory	Perspectives, experiences, aspirations Symbolic narrative	Symbolic narrative Best practices Creative generators System of organizational intelligence
To make decisions about . . .	Accommodating growth Administrative efficiency Managing failure	Direction based on political capital and expressed needs	Leadership selection Intervention strategies	Optimizing effectiveness
Comes into crisis when . . .	Adherents have options	Diversity inhibits generalization	Information floods cognitive and emotional functioning	Changes in the environment outstrip organizational learning

Figure 15.1 Organizational Stages and Information-Seeking Behavior by J. Russell Crabtree

be possible. Unfortunately, he is part of a culture formed around ordained leaders who do not seek this kind of information. While a portion of the resistance may be associated with a perceived threat to the ego, a large part may be attributed to a particular stage in the church's life where organizational intelligence is not valued.

Religious organizations are systems that evolve as they interact with their changing environments. Different environments require different organizational cultures, structures, and strategies, but they also require different information systems if they are to be effective. A leadership style that is out of sync with the environment it is called to serve will fail, not for want of purpose or goodness but because it is a two-pronged system in a three-pronged world. However, having a synced leadership style will not be adequate if the organization does not develop an information system that will provide the organizational intelligence required for effective action. The stages of that evolution and its corresponding information system are laid out in the model presented in figure 15.1 and described below.

The Instrumental Stage

In the instrumental stage the leader understands the organization as an extension of him- or herself. The leader's task is to develop a vision for the organization and then exercise the authority to direct the organization toward that vision. Due to a high degree of member loyalty, the leader functions without a sharp line between his or her own internal perspectives and those within the universe of the organization. The leader's primary task lies in constructing an administrative structure that operates in a relatively linear, cause-and-effect chain of action. The instrumental stage of leadership works well in contexts where options for members are limited. It also works well in short-term crisis situations found in emergency departments, fire departments, police departments, and the military.

The information sought at this stage focuses on assets that can be used to support the leader's vision. These tend to be objective in nature: members, money, and facilities. Since loyalty to a particular tradition and its positional proxy is paramount, there is little need to seek subjective information regarding the perspectives, experiences, and aspirations of members. In fact, a focus on these can be seen as hampering implementation of the leader's vision.

The instrumental stage begins to break down when institutional loyalty begins to erode. Information about membership, money, and facilities begins to indicate a downward trend, but that data alone provides few clues for a different course of action. If the leadership does not move forward to the next stage, it will keep trying to drum up support as its assets dwindle and by collecting as a matter of habit objective data that only documents its demise. The descriptor "cultural-religious alliance" in the figure refers to environments where the church and external culture are aligned in many respects. The blue laws of the 1950s are a classic example of this, but there are many others. This is what many people in the United States today are hankering to return to. When the church and external culture are aligned, people do not have as many choices (for example, all the stores are closed on Sunday). You have, in a sense, a monopoly. You don't have to pay much attention to the varied experiences folks are having.

The Generalizing Stage

In the generalizing stage the leader realizes the organization is not simply an extension of him- or herself. Members have their own views, which are distinct from the leader. Moreover, members have options. They can and will leave, taking their resources with them. Now the leader begins to pay more attention to what members think, but using an affiliative approach. Here, information flows to the leader through a set of relationships and is collected primarily through conversations. While these conversations represent a relatively small subset of the entire organization, the leader generalizes the information to reach conclusions about the entire body. The leader trusts his or her own powers of observation to assess the basic status of the organization. As these observations accumulate over time, the leader may become the institutional memory of the organization and members may defer to his or her understanding of where things stand.

The generalizing stage works well in small organizations where it is possible for the leader to have substantive conversations with nearly every member. It also works well in larger homogeneous organizations where a relatively small subset of members really does represent the views of the many. Where the rate of change within the organization is relatively low, episodic interactions spaced over time continue to be valid even though months or years may pass.

The generalizing stage begins to break down in larger, more diverse, and rapidly changing environments. Accustomed to the accuracy of the extrapolation of his or her own experiences across the entire organization, the leader begins to make mistakes. This can take the form of eruptions from people who do not feel that their perspectives, experiences, and aspirations are taken into account. In some cases the leader may find that he or she has really generalized a minority view and set out to lead based on that limited view, only to discover that hardly anyone is following. If the leadership does not move forward to the next stage, it will find itself asserting that it "knows what is going on" in an organization where, like a jack-in-the-box, surprises keep shooting up and hitting leaders on the chin.

The Neural Stage

In the neural stage, the leader begins to place less trust in his or her own immediate perceptions and seeks methods of collecting information that reliably represents the entire organization. This takes place particularly at moments when critical decisions need to be made that have a wide impact, especially the search for a new leader. The leader is confronted with a logistical challenge. Broad input is required to insure buy-in, but there may not be adequate time to have conversations with the numbers of people required to have reliable information that reflects the entire system.

Here the leader begins to engage a set of tools to supplement the conversational data, an organization-wide assessment. This generates a symbolic narrative, that is, the story of the entire system told using numbers as symbols of the perspectives, experiences, and aspirations of the membership. Such a symbolic narrative accommodates both the unity and the diversity of the body. It can be administered in a timely manner and it is repeatable. Using digital technology and benchmarking, the symbolic narrative can identify particular qualities, areas of strength and weakness, as well as reservoirs of energy and concern. In the neural stage, leaders begin to use this system-wide information episodically when major decisions need to be made. But as the information-gathering possibilities grow, so does the amount of information collected.

In the neural stage, the focus is on learning what is happening in the organization in an episodic fashion. But so much emphasis is placed on collecting information that inadequate attention is paid to how to use the information in a way that promotes effectiveness. The neural stage begins to break down as the leader begins to be overwhelmed with information. Expecting that information will actually make the hard decisions about what to do next, the leader instead finds that it simply raises more questions. If the leadership does not find a way to move to the next stage, the organization will fall into the well-known trap of analysis paralysis.

The Integrating Stage

In the integrating stage, the leader shifts from simply collecting more information to developing a system of organizational intelligence that will not only articulate needs and concerns but also identify and mobilize resources. Here, it is not the leader who becomes the answer to all the questions raised by the information system. *It is the learning of the system itself.* As the information system identifies elements of the organization that have discovered pathways to effectiveness and even best practices, these are celebrated and shared. In the integrating stage, this transparency is a value that is enacted and rewarded, whereas in other stages of a declining organization sharing effectiveness is discouraged, because it suggests an autonomy that is antithetical to the instrumental stage or a distinctiveness that is antithetical to the generalizing stage.

This approach to problem solving goes far beyond the simple brainstorming familiar to most leaders. In the integrating stage, information is synthesized with the creativity of the Spirit and the best practices from the larger church to develop a unique offering of the kingdom of God with its own mark and quality. If the larger system does not give enough support to experimentation, the changes in the environment will outstrip organizational learning and the system will revert to the neural stage.

Figure 15.1 refers to "effective outliers" as a context and "creative generators" as a way to seek information in this organizational stage. An effective outlier is someone who has discovered ways to be effective using nontraditional means. In previous stages, these people are marginalized. In the integrating stage, they are seen as resources to the larger system because they are learning some things that may be replicable. A creative generator is the person described in chapter 13 as an infopreneur.

Information Type as Filter

What is important about this model is that the types of information that are collected will define the organization and limit its development to the corresponding stage. This is not difficult to understand. The information type becomes the filter through which the organization sees itself and the world. Using the analogy of Sir Arthur Eddington, it is like using a fishing net with a three-inch mesh and concluding that there are no fish in the ocean smaller than three inches. Once a church decides what types of information it will collect, it determines what will be visible to it and to what it shall be blind. It is impossible to make a substantially different set of meaningful decisions regarding that which you cannot see.

A church at the *instrumental stage* that focuses on count data, that is, buildings, bucks, and bodies, sees the church through the filter of those metrics. These are the trip wires of concern and engagement. Other potential trip wires like plummeting morale or a loss of purpose are invisible to leaders in a church with this focus. The church will tend to attract and hold people for whom the decisive factor in their engagement is not the experience within the church but rather their commitment to the institution and the symbols that represent it. It will also attract and hold those who feel they have no other religious choices, either because of long-term emotional or social association or because the church is the sole avenue to salvation.

Conversely, a church at the instrumental stage will tend to bleed out those who value choices and subjective experience. When the church loses a purposeful verve, loyalty is not enough to hold them. Since the leadership has no feedback loops to gauge the quality of religious life that members are experiencing, there is no neural pathway to carry a pain signal from the body to the leadership. The information-seeking behavior that is focused on count data is decisive in maintaining a church at the instrumental stage.

A church at the *generalizing stage* focuses on conversational data and sees the church through the filter of the information that leaders are collecting through their communication with folks in their relational network. In this system, the anxieties of members in conversation with leaders become the trip wires of concern and engagement. Other potential trip wires that are system-wide rather than anecdotal are invisible to leaders with this focus. Since these leaders tend to generalize the import of their conversations over the entire body, it rarely occurs to leaders in a church at this stage that they do not have a good grasp on the whole. The information system they are using will guarantee the perpetuation of that error.

A church at the generalizing stage can make meaningful decisions that are relevant to the people represented in those conversations. It will tend to attract and hold people who value affiliations (it is about who you know), informal communication processes (grapevines), relational networks, long tenure, and corporate memory and who, above all, are willing to exert the energy to be heard. Conversely, it will tend to bleed out those who value engagement and impact outside of the relational power structure as well as those who have distinctive interests—for example, different age cohorts, whose unique perspectives are painted over by the generalizing brush. Two groups that are particularly vulnerable in a church at the generalizing stage are youth and young adults.

A church at the *neural stage* focuses on members' perspectives, experiences, and aspirations captured in symbolic narrative. A number of Episcopal dioceses, for example, have begun to use a standard, benchmarked assessment instrument communicated to every member of their congregations prior to searching for their next bishop. This represents a major step out of the generalizing stage, where information is collected from a relatively small number of people in focus groups, to the neural stage, where the input is received from many more, often over a thousand.

In the neural stage, leaders still see the church through information channeled to them through various relational networks, and the anxieties of members in the relational network continue to be the trip wires of engagement and concern. However, at critical moments in the church's life, such as a pastoral search or strategic planning, leaders provide a neural feedback loop by introducing opportunities for a more systematic assessment. Looking at the church through this filter on an episodic basis produces a series of snapshots that can reveal more texture and variety in the congregation's makeup that the generalizing tendencies tend to obscure. The church will attract people who value these opportunities for self-correction, but it may not want the higher levels of engagement that the integrating stage may require.

A church at the *integrating stage* also focuses on members' perspectives, experiences, and aspirations captured in symbolic narrative. However, now leaders see the church through the filter of the information coming to them through a cycle of intentional, system-wide, and reliable assessment processes. At this stage, significant declines in corporate vitality trigger concern and engagement, as do the unfulfilled aspirations and dreams of members that are revealed in the process. A church at the integrating stage will tend to attract and hold people that value energy and participation. It will especially attract leaders who value effectiveness and are motivated to grow by learning from others. Conversely, it will tend to bleed out those who value a more spectator role in the church as well as those who interpret the focus on subjective experience as pandering or failing to give adequate weight to tradition and authority.

In summary, the way that leaders go about collecting information determines how and what they can see as well as what is invisible to them. What is brought into their field of view is critical for the decisions they will make, who the church will attract and hold, and who it will lose in the process.

If a church at the integrating stage is going to deal effectively with organizational intelligence, it will need to make the organizational changes required to support it. That is the subject of the final chapter.

Discussion Questions

1. What information does your leadership team use to make decisions? From the description of the four organizational stages in the chapter, which stage do you think leaders in your church are in?

2. Organizations tend to stay in a particular stage until it stops working. What are some of the signs that a particular organizational stage is no longer working? Are those signs present in your church . . . or not?

3. What would be required for your leadership team to move to the next stage? What would have to change? What might be the benefits?

CHAPTER 16

Who Does Your Church's Organizational Intelligence?

So they brought him. When the spirit saw Jesus, it immediately
threw the boy into a convulsion. He fell to the ground and
rolled around, foaming at the mouth. Jesus asked the boy's
father, "How long has he been like this?"
—Mark 9:20-21

Fifteen years ago, if you would have asked most church leaders "Who does the church's IT?" you would have found yourself staring back into a puzzled face. Some would not know what you meant by IT. Some would understand what IT is, but would not know what it had to do with the church. A few would know what IT is and understand how it could benefit the church, but would respond with something like "No one does that for the church. We're not there yet." In 2011 most church leaders could name a person, either volunteer or staff, who handles the church's IT, website, email accounts, and so forth.

Today, you would receive a similar response to the question "Who does the church's OI (organizational intelligence)?" The overwhelming majority would not know what OI is. A few might know what it is, but not understand how it might benefit the church. Virtually no one would be able to provide a name for the person responsible for the church's OI.

Every church above one hundred people in worship needs an imbedded OI function with either a volunteer or a staff person charged with that responsibility. In this chapter I will outline the reasons.

Managing the OI Function in a Church

First, OI, like any ministry in the church, requires a particular gift mix. The necessary *abilities* include

- a capacity for helping people benefit from constructive feedback, both strengths and growth areas.
- a servant orientation that deals appropriately with the power of information.
- a level of comfort with basic mathematical operations and a willingness to learn some simple statistical functions.

From a *motivational* standpoint, people who are good candidates for OI in a church tend to

- enjoy solving puzzles and piecing together clues to arrive at a comprehensive picture.
- take pleasure in a process of discovery and being surprised by unexpected results.
- love spotting strengths and uncovering potential in people and groups.
- welcome opportunities to help people and groups identify what has them stuck so that they can move forward in a purposeful way.

Second, OI requires a consistent approach across the entire church. Just as churches do not want each group in the church disseminating information through its own version of the church's website, a church does not want groups collecting information using different, uncoordinated, and uneven approaches. I often hear pastors say that they cannot engage in a reliable, comprehensive assessment process because their members have been "surveyed to death," all by different groups with only pieces of the larger picture. The best way to insure consistency is to assign the OI function to a single individual or team.

I mentioned earlier that roughly 25 percent of the members in a typical church indicate that they often feel like they have something to give the church but do not know how to give it. Leaders can try to mine that potential by asking all ministry areas to redouble their efforts at recruitment. The other option is to use the OI function to get at the information in a more consistent manner. This does not require a massive computer database of gifts and interests. The OI person can simply survey the congregation on a quarterly basis and ask one question:

When you think about your relationship to your church, do you feel

- overutilized?
- underutilized?
- just right?

Upon receiving the stack of surveys, the OI person then takes a few simple actions.

- Discards the "just right" responses
- Sends the (few) "overutilized" responses to the pastor to deal with potential burnout
- Sends the "underutilized" responses to a volunteer coordinator who determines the best place to connect the people, given their gift mix and interests

By repeating this simple operation every three months, an OI function in a church can virtually reduce the number of underutilized members to zero, provide the names of people ready to make a contribution to various ministry areas eager to have them, avoid much of the duplication of effort found in uncoordinated recruitment methods, and utilize the gifts and interests of other OI people who may, themselves, be underutilized in the church.

Clearly, this is not rocket science. However, a church without an embedded OI function will generally not be able to consistently execute this simple but important process.

Third, OI requires a consistent application across time. Many times when I talk with folks about OI, they respond with, "Oh yes, we ran a survey last year." Running a survey is to OI what a snapshot is to a feature-length movie. Only by applying a consistent set of tools at appropriate time intervals can a church track progress, intersect entropy, identify shifts, make corrections, and celebrate growth. In many cases, it is difficult to understand what is happening without a longitudinal perspective.

Most of us are familiar with a genre of riddles like this one: A pipe, a carrot, and a couple sticks are lying together in a field. Why? Answer: They are what's left of a melted snowman.

What gives riddles of this sort their maddening quality is that they provide a single snapshot in time. It is difficult for the mind to construct a scenario out of the thousands of possibilities that could lead to such an outcome. A second photograph, taken with the same camera at the same location a week earlier (let's say), would have robbed the riddle of all its mystification.

Many times I am called in to help a church deal with a particular situation, and it is like looking at a pipe, a carrot, and a couple of sticks lying together in a field. Why? There is no earlier picture that helps me understand what has really happened. Talking with leaders often does not help. For example, in a conflict situation, it is natural to ask church leaders the question that Jesus asked of the boy's father in the Gospel of Mark, "How long has it been like this?"

Some leaders will claim that the conflict is episode based: "This all began last October when John Smith got a petition together to sell the parsonage!" But then I talk to other leaders who claim the conflict is long standing and system based: "This did not start in October! The church has been wrestling with the issue of the parsonage ever since the McCoy family donated the land to build it on an acre of their farm forty years ago!"

Which is it? It is not simply that I, as the outsider, am having trouble reconstructing what has happened. The leaders themselves do not know! Organizational intelligence gathered every three years using the same instrument would disclose the snowman and settle the question. Settling the question is important, because it is impossible to formulate a meaningful solution to a conflict that is poorly understood. Every conflict appears to be episode based, but in the organizational intelligence collected over time, we might discover one of the following:

- The church as a system is power-focused, with people feeling positive or negative about the ministries of the church depending upon which of three competing clans is in power at any particular time. The system generates episodes of conflict along these fault lines.
- The church as a system is clergy-focused, with people feeling positive or negative about the ministries of the church depending upon how they evaluate the work of the pastor. The church is also chaotic, having competing centers of energy that resist alignment to a leader or a vision. The system generates episodes of conflict centered on the pastor.
- The church as a system is both settled and aware of the need for change. The system generates episodes of conflict centered on its dissonance.
- The church as a system has a low level of tolerance combined with a conservative theological perspective. The system generates episodes of conflict centered on disagreements that are theologized as a conflict between good and evil.

These system-based issues are generally not clear to most people living in the midst of them, who tend to believe that the problems are caused by individual people or events. A robust OI function administered consistently over time will disclose them and make it more likely that the leaders can effectively intervene.

What Should Be Tracked?

There are two sets of intelligence that need to be tracked by the OI function in every church, three sets in a large church with a staff.

The first is represented by the congregation depicted in figure 16.1. There are more dimensions to the OI report, but for the sake of simplicity, only the energy-satisfaction map is discussed here. (Recall the figures in earlier chapters such as vitality status, member focus, critical success factors, level of criticality, and organizational culture.) The OI Track (represented by squares) in this chart tells an important story.

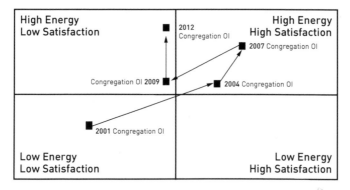

Figure 16.1. OI Track for a Congregation

In 2001, the church collected OI in preparation for a pastor search. The leaders discovered that the church was in the recovery quadrant (low energy, low satisfaction), which served as the occasion for a significant intervention. Armed with that OI, the church called a "good fit" pastor. Under her leadership the church moved into the transformational quadrant in 2004 and even deeper into the quadrant in 2007, after which she took another call. The next pastor arrived on the scene in 2008 and another collection of OI was conducted a year afterward in 2009. It was discovered that the church had experienced a significant drop in energy, which also served as the occasion of an intervention. A deeper look disclosed that the new pastor was much more settled in his worship style than the congregation, which was quite flexible, and this out-of-sync feeling was dropping the church's energy level. The pastor engaged the services of an experienced coach, made adjustments in his worship leadership style, and by 2012, the church's OI indicated a rebound.

I call this description the *ten-year intelligence narrative* of a church. The ten-year intelligence narrative is the witness data equivalent of the ten-year count profile every major denomination keeps on the finances, attendance, and membership of its churches. There are five reasons that a ten-year intelligence narrative is vital for leaders to have.

First, a ten-year intelligence narrative not only helps leaders know where a church *is* but also where it is coming *from*. In figure 16.1, leaders in 2004 might have been disappointed at the mediocre energy score from their OI. However, the 2001 OI shows that the church has emerged from the recovery quadrant, which constitutes progress to be celebrated.

Conversely, leaders in 2009 might have been satisfied with their OI until they realized that the church was actually in a pretty steep decline from where it had been in 2007. Where a church is coming from makes a tremendous difference in the action that is indicated. As Billy Graham used to say, "I would rather have one foot in hell headed toward heaven, than one foot in heaven headed toward hell."

Second, a ten-year intelligence narrative empowers leaders by lowering the threshold of engagement. Tracking the OI can help leaders engage issues before they are reflected in changes in worship attendance or giving. In his book *Leadership Is an Art*, Max De Pree asserts that one of the most challenging jobs of a leader is "the interception of entropy." Waiting until a drop in energy is reflected in a financial crisis that finally triggers engagement is often too late. Too many churches sitting in the recovery or static quadrants today are there because no one who could sound an alarm years before when the church had more options was tracking the OI.

Third, a ten-year intelligence narrative supports the development of the church as a learning organization. Tracking OI helps leaders identify what is working and not working. Someone has said that people tend to remember (and repeat) their mistakes and forget their lessons. An intelligence narrative helps a leadership team generate its own organizational *scriptures*, that is, a preserved record of lessons to be remembered.

Fourth, a ten-year intelligence narrative reliably represents what was happening across the entire church as opposed to an anecdotal narrative that may, or may not, accurately reflect the state of the church as a system. For example, an anecdotal narrative may identify a certain year as the date the new organ was installed, a high point. The OI tracking, on the other hand, may disclose that the energy level of a congregation took a dive during that time, because members were becoming spectators of what a relatively small group of others were doing.

Fifth, a ten-year intelligence narrative can help prospective leaders know if they are a good fit for a particular church. A tracking of OI can reveal that a church has lived in the transformation quadrant at some point in the past and may have transformation in its DNA that can be reactivated. Other churches may indicate a tendency to circle a vortex. For example, some churches are chronically chaotic, and since the best predictor of future behavior is past behavior, it is likely they will continue to be chronically chaotic. By knowing this in advance, a pastor can discern if he or she can flourish in such a system. At the very least, the OI can help alleviate self-blame when the church exhibits a tendency to circle back to its vortex.

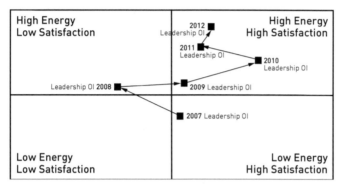

Figure 16.2. OI Track for the Leadership Team

The second set of OI that needs to be tracked is the state of the leadership team, which I would define narrowly as the pastor and board, but in some cases would also include other groups such as deacons, trustees, and executive committees. We see the OI track for a leadership team in figure 16.2.

Leadership OI needs to be collected every year, preferably midyear, due to the rotation of leaders on and off the board. In figure 16.2 the OI track reveals an overall growth pattern in the team's energy and satisfaction. There could be a number of factors influencing this movement, including these:

- The nominating process is doing a better job identifying candidates for the team.
- The pastor is doing a better job preparing leaders for their work.
- Leaders are learning how to work together as a team.
- The team is using the annual OI as an opportunity to continually improve their process.

All the reasons for tracking OI in congregations applies to the leadership team as well.

In large churches with staff, a third set of OI that needs to be tracked, also on an annual basis, is the status of the staff. In the OI track shown in figure 16.3, the staff appears to be circling a vortex in the static quadrant.

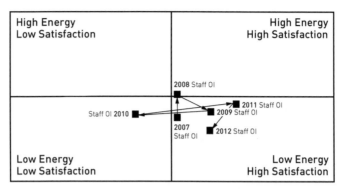

High Energy Low Satisfaction	High Energy High Satisfaction
Low Energy Low Satisfaction	Low Energy High Satisfaction

Figure 16.3. OI Track for the Staff

Whatever the specific reasons might be, several observations can be made from the OI track.

- The trend is long term and, most likely, difficult to change (though not impossible).
- The trend is independent of whatever changes have occurred due to staff turnover.
- The trend could be systemic, that is, driven by organizational structure or culture.
- The trend might point to a leadership issue.

Again, figure 16.3 is only one of many components in a staff OI report. It would be relatively easy to identify the driving factors in the rest of the intelligence.

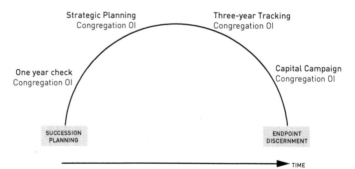

Figure 16.4. OI Track over the Pastoral Life Cycle

Finally, a fourth type of congregational OI should be collected for the pastoral life cycle, including major discernment points in the life of a congregation. These are illustrated in figure 16.4. A pastor begins work as the result of a succession process. A one-year check reveals areas of celebration as well as necessary corrections. Having established his or her leadership, the pastor is now prepared to work with the leadership team to refine the church's vision and establish tactics in a strategic plan. A three-year tracking cycle provides metrics on the implementation of the strategic plan. Long-term pastorates frequently include building expansion or renovation that requires a capital campaign. Eventually a pastor needs to discern whether it is time to stay and recommit or to seek the next call. All these discernment points in the pastoral life cycle are strengthened when they are informed by OI.

As with any other critical function within the body of Christ, the level of intentionality in generating and using OI in evidence-based discernment cannot be accomplished apart from an imbedded OI function. Just as a church needs someone who does the church's IT, it also needs someone or some group dedicated to doing the church's OI. In addition, leaders must be trained to apply the intelligence in their ministries. That is the topic of another book.

When it comes to knowing how members are actually experiencing the church, the body of Christ, the church should do a better job than any other organization in the world, not by avoiding information but by our peculiar ability as Christians to weave the gospel into everything we do and to turn knowledge and insight into a love that abounds.

Discussion Questions

1. Who does the IT work in your church? Describe the process by which your church began to take IT seriously. How might the introduction of OI follow the same path?

2. Many mainline churches can easily access ten years of count data on their church: membership, worship attendance, giving, expenditures, involvement in education, and so forth. The witness data for the organizational intelligence is totally missing. Suppose you as a leader had ten years of organizational intelligence as discussed in this book? How might that be useful?

3. If you were to appoint a small group of members to develop organizational intelligence for the church, who might they be? How would you want them to get started? How would you present it to the church?

Conclusion

I began this book citing organizational intelligence from the emergency department of a major children's hospital indicating that 75 to 85 percent of those who bring a child to the emergency department feel positive about the experience. Here is the rest of the story. Several years earlier, those same scores were among the worst of any hospital in the country. There were, of course, the predictable bruised egos and special pleadings, but to the credit of the leadership team, they chose to trust their instruments. Upon closer inspection, the data revealed a clear pattern, which identified two factors critical to improving the quality of care: (1) reduce the level of pain that children experienced during procedures and (2) do a better job keeping parents informed regarding what was happening.

The department leadership took two steps to address these issues. First, they instituted a No Pain Campaign, with the goal of eliminating all pain from procedures administered to children. This included the application of a topical ointment fifteen minutes prior to any needle stick (injection, blood draw, IV placement) that made those procedures virtually painless for the child. Second, they instituted a rounding policy, where a staff member checks in with parents every twenty minutes to see how they and the child are doing and to relay information about the status of any tests, procedures, treatments, and so forth. With the institution of these two steps, the rating of the hospital by parents rocketed from among the lowest in the country to one of the highest. In fact, the emergency department has been ranked as the best emergency department for children in the entire country. They did not have to change everything. They simply needed to change the right things.

Does this make a difference? Imagine that you, as a parent, wake up one morning to the cries of your child, who is experiencing a significant amount of pain. You have a choice of two hospitals, both equal in medical skill. However, one will take steps to insure that your child has virtually no pain from any procedures and will keep you fully apprised of everything that is happening every twenty minutes. Which choice would you make?

Whether we like it or not, whether it fits our doctrinal theories or ecclesiastical loyalty, people have the same kind of choice regarding churches, some of which exhibit chronic dissatisfaction and loss of purpose, others that give new meaning to the lives of all who enter them.

The same quality of organizational intelligence that helped transform this emergency department is now available to churches, middle judicatories, regional associations, and Christian schools through tools that are affordable and easy to administer. We can now gain a clear understanding of the quality of member experiences in our churches and the critical factors for improving them. For those who assert that a church is not a hospital, I would contend that a hospital should be our minimum standard. The words *salvation* and *salve* have the same root. When I interview members from transformational churches, one theme I hear is summed up in this truth-ringing statement: "This church helped me get over my bad Jesus trips from other churches." The church should be second to none in caring for the souls of people, and that includes an unflinching assessment of the degree to which people are experiencing the body of Christ as a milieu that generates peace and energy.

Imagine a church where all congregations are transformational, and, regardless of size or setting, are engaged in effective strategies of replication, expansion, and external impact—in their community, nationally, globally. Imagine that they have the organizational intelligence that can help them not change everything but the right things. What would it be like if congregations could face the spiritual dissonances that keep sabotaging their best efforts and setting up their leaders for failure? What would it be like if congregations could identify their unique operating systems and the approaches to ministry that are likely to be effective for them—and which are not, regardless of how well they have worked in other places? Imagine that the same intelligence could help leaders manage their pastoral transitions in a way that is tailored to who they are, with minimal disruption to their mission, and call a next pastor who is a good fit for them. Imagine financial campaigns that are grounded in reality and shaped by what is important to folks in a particular congregation rather than an out-of-the-box approach that generates frustration and fatigue. Imagine the checkups that we do annually for our physical bodies to catch problems early, but conducted with the body of Christ so that we can address problems at a point prior to the entire system falling into chaos, static, or recovery states.

For that incredible creature that is the namesake of this book, owl sight is not an optional ability that makes life interesting; it is key to his survival. Without it, he is destined to the scraps of food left by others on the forest floor. For the effective church leader in the information age, organizational intelligence is not optional either. It offers the capacity to see more clearly into the hearts of people to lead them to love and serve God at a time when other powers have far less noble purposes in mind.

This is the promise of evidence-based discernment. I know it is possible because it is already happening! I am leading a movement called Project iSight. If you are interested in learning more about Project iSight, please contact me.

J. Russell Crabtree, President
Holy Cow! Consulting
PO Box 8422
Columbus, Ohio 43201-8422
www.holycowconsulting.com
russ@holycowconsulting.com
614-208-4090

Per aspera, ad astra.
Through difficulty to the stars.
Epiphany 2012

Appendix A

Glossary

anecdotally-driven processes	decision processes that rely on conversations with individuals or groups who do not necessarily represent the entire church
authority-driven processes	decision processes that rely on the perspectives of those in positions of power in hierarchical systems
chaotic state or system	a church with multiple, competing centers of energy not aligned to a central purpose
clergy-focused church	a church where members base their view of the entire church's ministry on some aspect of the clergy's work performance
count data	information that can be obtained by simply counting people or things
critical success factor	an unfulfilled longing among members regarding some element of the church's ministry
criticality	the level of urgency indicated for the critical success factors of a church
energy	a compelling purpose or message combined with a high level of engagement (in contrast to simply watching others or going through the motions of religious activity)
evidence-based discernment	a discovery process that integrates core values, organizational intelligence, and an inspired imagination
expert-driven processes	decision processes that rely on the wisdom and knowledge resident in the mind of a highly respected and insightful individual
flexibility	the basic disposition of a church relative to change
generalizing stage	an organizational stage where the leader acquires information about the church through a set of relationships
Hearth and Home culture	a church culture ultimately concerned with a clearly defined faith that is lived out in a community valuing structure and stability (Shadow side: critical spirit, system bound)

implicit pattern	a pattern in the life of a congregation that cannot be discovered by count data alone, is difficult to identify through traditional meetings, is not intuitively obvious, and has important long-term implications
impression-driven processes	decision processes that rely on the internal thoughts and feelings of the people in leadership roles to gauge reality
instrumental stage	an organizational stage where the leader understands the church as an extension of him- or herself
integrating stage	an organizational stage where the leader develops a system of organizational intelligence that fosters the emergence of a learning system
leadership clarity	the degree to which members have a shared and accurate understanding of the perspectives, experiences, and aspirations of the members they lead and serve
Magi culture	a church culture ultimately concerned with the rational integrity of their faith, the just application of faith to life, and the journey of understanding and discovery (Shadow side: lack of boundaries)
member focus	the lens that members are using to determine how they feel about the church overall (clergy-focused, power-focused, ministry-focused)
ministry-focused church	a church where members evaluate how they feel about the church overall based upon various ministries
neural stage	an organizational stage where the leader relies on organization-wide assessment through a set of tools that supplement conversational data
OI	shorthand for organizational intelligence
operating system	the ideas, language, values, rewards, and penalties experienced in a church that are decisive in the success or failure of ministry initiatives
organizational culture	the set of values and repeated behaviors in a church created by the interplay between theological perspective and flexibility
organizational intelligence	the information that is critical to understanding a church comprising both count data and witness data
Paraclete culture	a church culture that is ultimately concerned with the development of communities that are intellectually open and reflective, but with attention paid to the importance of structure and ritual (Shadow side: compassion fatigue, lack of accountability)
Performance culture	a church culture ultimately concerned with an experiential faith presented in a way that people find accessible and compelling (Shadow side: lack of depth and authenticity)

power-focused church	a church where members base their view of the entire church's ministry on the leadership team's performance
recovery state or system	a church struggling to rediscover a clear purpose and sense of wholeness in its life and ministry
satisfaction	an expansive term that includes completeness, wholeness, health, peace, welfare, safety, soundness, tranquility, prosperity, perfectness, fullness, rest, harmony, and the absence of agitation or discord
spiritual dissonance	the church's experience when it desires two things that are fundamentally exclusive of one another
static state or system	a church where members feel generally positive in spite of the fact that the church's life is not sustainable
transformational state or system	a church with the demonstrated capacity to positively impact those within the church and the community it serves
vitality status	the state of the church as defined by the level of satisfaction and energy experienced by members
witness data	information that can only be gathered when a person speaks

Appendix B

Tools and Tips for Generating Organizational Intelligence

With the advent of information technology, generating organizational intelligence is straightforward and relatively inexpensive. However, obtaining reliable information requires the use of well-designed and tested instruments. Leaders are often tempted to design their own tools. There are a number of reasons not to do this, including the following:

1. Survey design requires expertise.

Survey design and administration requires some basic knowledge if you are going to obtain results that are reliable enough to make important decisions.

This begins with knowing what you should measure. Do you measure programs? Attitudes? Behaviors? Then you need to decide what scale to use. Yes-no? Disagree-agree? Should you rank items? Or rate them?

There are issues of administration. How do you get a good response rate? How many is enough?

Finally, there is the issue of analysis. Do you only want frequency counts? Percentages? Where do you need the data broken down by categories such as age, gender, involvement, and so forth? What correlations do you need to run?

2. Survey design is time consuming.

Even with the right expertise, a committee of three or four people generally finds designing a survey from scratch to be a very time-consuming endeavor. This can be avoided by assigning the work to one person, but this negates what a church is often trying to accomplish by designing its own survey in the first place: an instrument with broad input.

And after the survey questions are crafted and the instrument is formatted and printed (or posted on the Internet), you still have the work of distributing it, publicizing it, doing the data entry, and analysis.

3. Survey processing requires special software.

A number of steps in survey administration require special software.

If you are going to post the instrument on the Web, you have to have a server that will host that for you.

If you run a print survey, you will need data entry software and a check program. (Reliable data entry requires a double entry, which creates two files that are then checked against each other.)

After the data entry, a statistical analysis will need to be conducted. This either requires a person with a statistical package such as SPSS-PC or SAS or a person with an advanced knowledge of spreadsheets.

4. Survey design is expensive.

Designing your own survey not only requires considerable volunteer labor but also generally requires significant staff support. This usually amounts to twenty hours of work or more just to generate the survey and bring it to a point where it can be distributed. Additional staff time may be required for data entry and report generation. Many leaders have calculated the cost of developing their own survey and have concluded that it will cost the organization two to three times the price of purchasing our service.

5. You may not know what your survey data means.

After you receive your results, you may not know if a given score is high or low. For example, if 60 percent of respondents indicate they are generally satisfied, is that good or not? If 10 percent of respondents indicate they are disturbed by the level of conflict, is that a problem, or is that just the way it is in churches?

The instruments provided by Holy Cow! Consulting have been developed with input from a large number of people across your organization type: congregation, regional association, church camp, college, primary or secondary school, staff, leadership board. The instruments have a track record of effectiveness. They come with step-by-step instructions and technical support. And with a large database behind each one, we know what is typical, what is to be celebrated, and what is a potential problem.

For Churches

A number of companies have developed high quality tools for generating organizational intelligence. Some of the tools developed by Holy Cow! Consulting and referenced in this book are listed below.

TOOL LOGO AND NAME	PURPOSES
Leadership Clarity Check©	To help leadership teams (board, clergy, program staff) evaluate the degree to which they share a common understanding of the perspectives, experiences, and aspirations of the members they lead and serve.
	Succession and strategic planning
CAT **Church Assessment Tool©** **Vital Signs©**	To help leadership teams achieve clarity regarding the vitality, culture, critical success factors, and priorities of the church through the eyes of members.
	Succession and strategic planning, preparation for search, financial campaigns, vocational discernment, benchmarking
Pulse©	To help leadership teams achieve clarity regarding the vitality, culture, critical success factors of a church staff through the eyes of staff members.
	Succession and strategic planning, preparation for search, financial campaigns, vocational discernment, benchmarking, team building
Conversations©	To help leadership teams achieve clarity regarding the vitality, culture, and priorities of a church with fewer than 35 people in worship.
	Strategic planning, preparation for search, vocational discernment, benchmarking
Family Tree©	To help new senior leaders at start-up in understanding the relational networks of the church.
	Succession planning—start-up
FocalPoints©	To help a leadership team, clergy and lay, gauge how well they are functioning.
	Benchmarking, performance review, mutual ministry review
FreshLook©	To help a clergyperson discern if his or her current position continues to be a good fit or if it is time to seek another call.
	Vocational discernment

For Regional Associations—Synods, Dioceses, Presbyteries, Conferences

TOOL LOGO AND NAME	PURPOSES
Leadership Clarity Check©	To help leadership teams (board, clergy, staff) evaluate the degree to which they share a common understanding of the perspectives, experiences, and aspirations of the church leaders in their jurisdiction. Succession and strategic planning
Portal© **Landscape©**	To help leadership teams achieve clarity regarding the vitality, culture, critical success factors, and priorities of the regional association through the eyes of local church leaders. Succession and strategic planning, preparation for search, financial campaigns, benchmarking
Pulse©	To help leadership teams achieve clarity regarding the vitality, culture, critical success factors of a church staff through the eyes of staff members. Succession and strategic planning, preparation for search, financial campaigns, vocational discernment, benchmarking, team building
FocalPoints©	To help the leadership team of a regional association, clergy and lay, gauge how well they are functioning. Benchmarking, performance review, mutual ministry review
i **iSight©**	Provide system of information that empowers synods, presbyteries, dioceses, and conferences to serve a transformational role in their congregations by improving their ability to manage the interactions and interventions through organizational intelligence. Benchmarking, tracking, clergy placement, outplacement, coaching

For Christian Schools, Colleges, and Universities

TOOL LOGO AND NAME	PURPOSES
Leadership Clarity Check©	To help leadership teams (board, headmaster, president) evaluate the degree to which they share a common understanding of the perspectives, experiences, and aspirations of the administration, faculty, and parents. Succession and strategic planning
Listening Post© **Intel©**	To help leadership teams achieve clarity regarding the strengths, critical success factors, and priorities as seen through the eyes of parents, faculty, administration, and board. Succession and strategic planning, preparation for search
FocalPoints©	To help the leadership team of a school (headmaster, president, and board) gauge how well they are functioning. Benchmarking, performance review

For more information on these tools, go to www.holycowconsulting.com/churches.

Notes

Introduction

1. Steve Lohr, "The Age of Big Data," *The New York Times*, February 11, 2012.

Chapter 1

1. Johann Wolfgang von Goethe, "Until One Is Committed," *Rag and Bone Shop of the Heart*, ed. Robert Bly, James Hillman, and Michael Meade (New York: HarperCollins, 1992), 235.
2. For a fuller treatment of specialism see J. Russell Crabtree, "The Trinity as an Antidote to Specialism," *Fly in the Ointment* (New York: Church Publishing, 2008), 26.

Chapter 2

1. Andrew Newberg and Mark Robert Waldman, *How God Changes Your Brain: Breakthrough Findings from a Leading Neuroscientist* (New York: Ballantine Books, 2009), 5.

Chapter 3

1. Bill Hybels, "We Were Wrong!" *Christianity Today* blog, October 24, 2007, http://heresyhunter.blogspot.com/2007/10/bill-hybels-we-were-wrong.html.
2. This research has been conducted using an instrument originally called the Church Planning Questionnaire, which was developed in 1974 by Dr. Grayson Tucker while serving as the dean of Louisville Presbyterian Seminary. The survey was developed under the guidance and inspiration of Dr. Ronald Lippitt, professor emeritus of sociology and psychology at the University of Michigan, who encouraged Tucker to integrate the learnings of organizational research with the operations of the church. The research work of Dean Hoge, professor of sociology at the Catholic University of America, also provided impetus for a more intentional evaluation of congregational health. The Church Planning Questionnaire was one result of those influences.

The church planning questionnaire was developed to meet the following criteria:

- It should serve both Roman Catholic and Protestant congregations.
- It should reflect the climate of the church rather than a lengthy evaluation of every program of the church, with the understanding that a positive church climate creates a field of health that is conducive to and reflective of effective programming.
- It should register the particular theological orientation of the congregation and the way faith functions in its life rather than focus solely on operational issues.
- It should not only capture a snapshot of the current state of the church, it should also include the priorities for a preferred future.
- It should provide a method for normalizing the data in order to determine what is typical, what is exceptional, and what is problematic.
- In setting norms, it should recognize the dynamics of church size and that different-sized churches have different characteristics.
- It should provide a way to computerize the data so that relationships between portions of the survey could be explored.
- It should allow for customization of the survey to address issues facing particular congregations.

To date, the Church Planning Questionnaire has been used with hundreds of churches from ten different denominations, including Baptist, Disciples of Christ, Episcopal, Presbyterian, Roman Catholic, and United Methodist, in eighteen different states.

In 1983, the findings from one hundred churches were compiled by Tucker and published in the book *The Church Planning Questionnaire: Manual and Discoveries from 100 Churches.* In that book, Tucker compares his findings with other researchers, including Carl Dudley, Wade Clark Roof, Lyle E. Schaller, and George Gallup.

After Tucker's retirement, the work with the questionnaire was continued by me. I have both served as a pastor and worked as a researcher in industry. I updated the computer report generated by the questionnaire to include graphics and narrative text and named it "Vital Signs." This church assessment tool has been used systematically by regional bodies with churches in transition and continues to be an important tool for churches doing strategic planning.

The questionnaire was significantly revised and updated in 2006 to reflect an increased emphasis on worship and music, the diversity of church styles, the ministry of the laity, the leadership of the pastor, and the importance of lifelong learning.

Chapter 4

1. If I remember correctly, this story is from psychologist Lawrence LeShan. However, in researching its source, I have thus far been unable to confirm my recollection.
2. Dietrich Bonhoeffer, *Life Together* (New York: Harper & Row, 1954), 107.
3. Allan W. Wicker, "Attitudes Versus Actions: The Relationship of Verbal and Overt Behavioral Responses to Attitude Objects," *Journal of Social Issues* 25, no. 4 (1969): 41–78.
4. See *Rational Christian Thinking*, chapter 1 (Cincinnati, OH: Equipping Ministries International, 1990), 4.

Chapter 5

1. *Straddled pastoral leadership* means a single pastor serving two very different congregations and there is no attempt to merge or unite them. The pastor straddles the fence to serve them both, but doesn't try to knock the fence down in the short term. *Segmented pastoral leadership* refers to two pastors serving two different congregations under the same governance structure, with some responsibilities shared across the two congregations and some segmented to a particular congregation.

Chapter 7

1. Sir Arthur Conan Doyle, "The Adventure of Silver Blaze," *The Strand Magazine: An Illustrated Monthly*, Vol. 4, July–December 1892, 656–57.
2. See note 2 in chapter 3 for background information on the origins and development of this database.
3. The data has been accumulated over thirty-five years of work with congregations using the church assessment tool "Vital Signs" (see note 2 in chapter 3).
4. The research for this data was conducted by Holy Cow! Consulting in 2011 from a sample of data collected from thirty congregations using the church assessment tool "Vital Signs."

Chapter 8

1. Helmut Thielicke, *The Evangelical Faith*, vol. 2, *The Doctrine of God and of Christ*, 227.
2. John Calvin, *The Library of Christian Classics*, vol. 20, *Calvin: Institutes of the Christian Religion*, ed. John T. McNeil (Philadelphia: Westminster Press, 1955) 36.

Chapter 9

1. See note 2 in chapter 3 for information about "Vital Signs," the church assessment tool referred to throughout this book.
2. Ibid.

Chapter 11

1. Lawrence LeShan, *Cancer as a Turning Point,* rev. ed. (New York: Penguin Books, 1994), 23.
2. Ibid., 41.
3. George Ainsworth-Land, "New Rules for Growth and Change," in *The Leader-Manager,* ed. John Williamson (New York: John Wiley & Sons, 1984), 146.
4. In reality, a few people indicate they will become less involved, but a larger number indicate they will become more involved. If we subtract the percentage of people who indicate they will become less involved from those who indicate they will become more involved, the net result is about 20 percent.

Chapter 14

1. This information comes from the use of the portal administered to about ten thousand people in fifteen different regional associations. The *Portal*® is a benchmarked assessment instrument developed by Holy Cow! Consulting especially for middle judicatories like dioceses, presbyteries, and synods that are seeking clarity regarding the perspectives, experiences, and aspirations of their people.

About the Author

J. Russell Crabtree is an Ohio native and graduate of The Ohio State University with a degree in engineering physics. He worked in research at the Eastman Kodak company for three years in the area of optics and electrostatic control systems. He left industry to attend seminary and served as a pastor for twenty years. In 1998 Russ founded and served for five years as the executive director of Montaña de Luz, a project providing hospice care for abandoned children with HIV-AIDS in Honduras. In the wake of Hurricane Mitch he founded and directed Ohio Hurricane Relief for Central America. He is the cofounder and president of Holy Cow! Consulting, which provides strategic planning, training, and organizational assessment. He also founded and directs BestMinds, a company specializing in awareness and intervention training for suicide and domestic violence. He has worked with cross-professional teams in counties with high suicide rates to develop prevention and intervention strategies; he helped shape the suicide prevention plan developed by the state of Ohio.

Russ has extensive experience in assisting organizations across the United States with strategic planning, mediation, customer surveys, and training. He has worked with many different organizations, including churches, libraries, colleges, and an arboretum. He has developed training for organizations in strategic planning, conflict management, team building, staff morale, customer service, and enhancing board function.

As a Presbyterian pastor, Russ served in small, midsize, and large churches in New York and Ohio. In that role, he was active in his regional association (presbytery) and worked in the areas of strategic planning, energy conservation, human sexuality, church consultation, presbytery staffing, and administrative oversight. He has served as a consultant to presbyteries and the Episcopal Church at both the national and diocesan level in the areas of training, succession planning, conflict management, and congregational assessment.

He has developed congregational and regional association assessment tools and has maintained a substantial database on church characteristics and congregations of all sizes and contexts. He is the creator of Portal®, an assessment instrument for regional associations; Pulse®; a staff climate assessment tool for larger churches and regional associations, and FocalPoints®, an assessment tool for boards and leadership teams. He has developed a number of products for churches in transition.

With Carolyn Weese, Russ coauthored *The Elephant in the Board Room: Developing a Pastoral Succession Plan for Your Church*, published in August 2004. The concepts of this book have been incorporated in a workbook developed to assist church leaders in pastoral succession planning. Using these materials he has assisted some of the largest churches in the United States in developing succession plans. In 2008 he published *The Fly in the Ointment: Why Denominations Aren't Helping Their Churches and How They Can.*

Other works include *Mountain of Light, The Story of Montana de Luz*, published in April 2005, and *A Second Day*, published in May 2008.

Russ has four children and lives with his wife, Shawn, in Temple, Texas.

For further information contact:

J. Russell Crabtree
Holy Cow! Consulting
PO Box 8422
Columbus, Ohio 43201
614-208-4090
russ@holycowconsulting.com
www.holycowconsulting.com